THE
AMRITSAR
MASSACRE

THE BRITISH EMPIRE'S WORST ATROCITY

THE
AMRITSAR
MASSACRE

THE BRITISH EMPIRE'S WORST ATROCITY

VANESSA HOLBURN

PEN & SWORD
HISTORY

AN IMPRINT OF PEN & SWORD BOOKS LTD.
YORKSHIRE – PHILADELPHIA

First published in Great Britain in 2019 by
PEN AND SWORD HISTORY
An imprint of
Pen & Sword Books Ltd
Yorkshire – Philadelphia

Hardback: 978 1 52674 577 4
Paperback: 978 1 52675 146 1

A CIP catalogue record for this book is available from the British Library.

Typeset in Times New Roman 11.5/14 by
Aura Technology and Software Services, India
Printed and bound in England by CPI Group (UK) Ltd, Croydon, CR0 4YY

Pen & Sword Books Limited incorporates the imprints of Atlas, Archaeology,
Aviation, Discovery, Family History, Fiction, History, Maritime, Military, Military
Classics, Politics, Select, Transport, True Crime, Air World, Frontline Publishing,
Leo Cooper, Remember When, Seaforth Publishing, The Praetorian Press,
Wharncliffe Local History, Wharncliffe Transport, Wharncliffe True Crime and
White Owl.

For a complete list of Pen & Sword titles please contact
PEN & SWORD BOOKS LIMITED
47 Church Street, Barnsley, South Yorkshire, S70 2AS, England
E-mail: enquiries@pen-and-sword.co.uk
Website: www.pen-and-sword.co.uk

Or
PEN AND SWORD BOOKS
1950 Lawrence Rd, Havertown, PA 19083, USA
E-mail: Uspen-and-sword@casematepublishers.com
Website: www.penandswordbooks.com

Contents

Foreword

This year is the centenary of the Jallianwala Bagh Massacre, or the Amritsar Massacre as it is better known in the UK, and I cannot think of a better time for this important study of the event to be published or of anyone more qualified to write it than Vanessa. The Amritsar Massacre cannot be over-imbued with importance in the struggle for independence. Gandhiji and other leaders saw the massacre as evidence that there could not be a liberal empire, and that the only way for Indians, Pakistanis and Bangladeshis to live with dignity and freedom was in an independent country free of Britain. The actions of General Dyer and the British Raj on that day began the final inexorable march to independence that we celebrate every year on 15th August.

I remember my childhood in Punjab, growing up in the region that suffered one of the most heinous acts of colonial repression suffered in British India. I was mere miles from Amritsar and remember from a young age visiting the Jallianwala Bagh, seeing the pockmarked walls where bullets had hit hard stone rather than soft flesh and peering into the dark well that hundreds had sought refuge in from the crack of rifle fire. It left a deep and lasting impression on my soul and has informed my work as an MP against oppression, intolerance and racism. We knew families in villages around us that had lost loved ones, parents and grandparents who had been there and lived through the ensuing repression. It stung the hearts of those in the Punjab and across India even then.

Today, the Amritsar Massacre still looms large in the Indian psyche and millions still partly define the UK through this prism. Sadly, millions of British school children do not even know what the Amritsar Massacre is, never mind the effect it continues to this day to have on our country's foreign relations. In this the centenary year, I would like to see the British Government again recognize the role it played in the terrible violence that day and take steps to keep the memory of that singularly terrible act alive. I believe we need to have a permanent memorial to the massacre in London, the heart of the British Empire, which will then also act as a memorial to other acts of colonial oppression that have gone unremembered more broadly. I also want to see the Amritsar Massacre become a key part of the curriculum. The history of colonialism is a key part of British history and not one that should be erased. It should be taught across the country as part of lessons on the creation of the modern United Kingdom. I do not want to drive division, distrust and hatred; Britain and India have much to gain from one another, and so much in common. They are the most natural of allies and friends in the modern world, but we must honour those that went before and we do a disservice to today's young if we don't prepare them with the lessons of the past.

Virendra Sharma
Member of Parliament for Ealing Southall

Introduction

On 13 April 1919, Indian-born British army officer General Reginald Dyer strode into the Jallianwala Bagh in the Punjab city of Amritsar and ordered his riflemen to fire on an unarmed crowd. The shooting, lasting around ten minutes, used 1,650 rounds of ammunition and left at least 379 civilian natives dead, with many more wounded. There was no warning issued before the troops opened fire and no medical aid given to the injured and dying; in fact afterwards many were left in agony overnight as a city-wide curfew was imposed. The Jallianwala was a public garden of six to seven acres, completely enclosed by high walls, with only a few very narrow exits available to the crowd; exits that were not large enough for the crowd to disperse quickly. Many who had gathered there that day were simply resting, after visiting the holy city and its temple during the Sikh festival of *Baisakhi*. The bullets killed Sikhs, Muslims and Hindus, pilgrims and political speakers, farmers, traders and merchants, men, women and children. The youngest victim was just six weeks old.

This massacre has caught the attention of film producers and authors in recent years – perhaps displaying how our modern eyes can barely believe that these actions took place in the name of British rule. In 1981, British Indian novelist Salman Rushdie portrayed the massacre in his book *Midnight's Children*, from the perspective of a doctor in the crowd, saved from the gunfire by a well-timed sneeze, with images of the massacre making it into the 2012 film adaptation directed by Indo-Canadian Deepa Mehta. It was also depicted in Richard Attenborough's 1982 critically acclaimed film *Gandhi*, with Edward Fox cast as General Dyer, along with scenes from the Hunter inquiry, which investigated the event. In 1984, in the TV series *The Jewel in the Crown*, the fictional widow of a British officer who is haunted by the inhumanity of the massacre tells how she came to be reviled because she refused to sympathise with Dyer, instead donating money to Indian victims. In Bali

Rai's 2009 novel, *City of Ghosts*, fictional stories come to a head on the day of the Amritsar Massacre, with references to Dyer and to Udham Singh, who would go on to assassinate Sir Michael O'Dwyer, Lieutenant Governor of the Punjab, and Reginald Dyer's superior officer. Most recently, in 2014, period drama *Downton Abbey* made a reference to the massacre as 'that terrible Amritsar business'. While some characters express their disapproval over the shooting, some support it. The event continues to divide opinion today.

Dyer had taken charge of Amritsar after days of civil unrest and violence, which were the result of the arrest and deportation of two nationalist leaders, the Hindu Dr Satya Pal and Dr Saifuddin Kitchlew, a Muslim, who were both supporters of Gandhi's passive resistance philosophy. Gandhi himself had been taken from a train and arrested prior to his arrival in Amritsar. The Deputy Commissioner of the Punjab, Miles Irving, handed over the city to the military fearing that he could not contain the spreading violence that had seen Europeans killed and attacked, and civil buildings ransacked. However, for the two days immediately before the Jallianwala Bagh massacre, Amritsar had been quiet with the populace accepting a lock down and ban on gatherings. Immediately after the shooting, Amritsar was placed under a tyrannical martial law, dished out by over zealous soldiers. It was during this time that the humiliation of the Crawling Order was imposed on city inhabitants. The infamous punishment meant that anyone who wished to pass through a road that had been the scene of an attack on a British woman was forced to crawl along the whole length of the street on his or her belly.

The unrest was not isolated to Amritsar but mirrored across the Punjab. The region was of particular importance to the British as it was home to the railways that served the North West frontier, was an important trading hub – and had provided rich pickings for Indian Army recruitment. Sir Michael O'Dwyer, who had grown up in Tipperary, against a backdrop of home-rule troubles, was a known hardliner when it came to the rule of the British Raj. O'Dwyer supported Dyer's actions at the time and continued to do so when Dyer was later investigated and criticised. As time went on, both Dyer and O'Dwyer were asked to explain and justify the manner in which the unrest in Amritsar and the Punjab was dealt with. Dyer cast himself as the hero of the hour – putting down the insurgence before it spread further – to the benefit of the rest of the region and India itself. Much of British India supported this version of events.

Eventually, enough concern was raised over the incident, and the months of military occupation that followed it, to force the British Government to push its Indian counterpart to investigate. In October 1919, the Government of India announced an Inquiry into the disturbances in Bombay, Delhi and the Punjab. The Disorder Inquiry Committee – or the 'Hunter Committee' as it came to be known – was tasked with examining the causes of the unrest – and the measures taken to counter it. Former MP and judge Lord Hunter chaired the Committee. There were a further four British and three Indian members. While hopes were high at the beginning of the process – particularly as Lord Hunter had no imperial connections and the Committee was thorough with questioning – many were unhappy with the one-sided evidence it examined. Dyer was perhaps shockingly honest at the Inquiry – he clearly lived a blinkered existence, believing that a British military officer was beyond criticism, particularly when any opposition came from Indians.

By March 1920, the two hundred-page Hunter Report sat on Viceroy Chelmsford's desk. Despite his experience in colonial politics, with the roles of governor of both Queensland and New South Wales on his CV, Chelmsford must have despaired, having used waiting for the findings as an excuse to delay taking any action. The Committee had failed to reach a unanimous verdict and instead the opinions were split along racial divides, with the Indian members of the Committee producing their own 'minority report'. Both sides had however agreed that Dyer was wrong not to offer a warning before he gave the order to shoot, that the firing continued for an unnecessarily long time and that Dyer overstepped his authority by firing to create a wider 'moral effect'. Next it was the turn of the Viceroy's Legislative Council to decide what to do about the shooting, and that was no easy task, since here too, members disagreed widely with each other.

Eventually, it was decided merely to remove Dyer from his post and not to offer him any future employment in the army. Dyer was asked to resign and did so. He was not to be charged or punished further, both because if he was charged and found innocent there could be further civil unrest and if he were punished, it could likely affect the morale of all serving soldiers. This approach was an attempt to appease every side of the debate. But since, as the adage warns, you can't please all of the people, all of the time, it was doomed to fail.

When Dyer returned to England, it was to court controversy. He was supported by many – including superior officers such as O'Dwyer, Conservative MPs, the *Morning Post* newspaper and more importantly by the military members of the Army Council. Dyer fought his case on the basis that he had been judged without ever receiving a trial. He also became a political pawn between Liberals and Indian reformists and those connected to British India who were determined to maintain the Empire at any cost. The ongoing debate ripped through the Commons, where the Liberal government gained the upper hand, and the more Conservative Lords, where those with vested interests in the status quo and the military humiliated the Liberals. While the disputes had no practical outcome, the impact would be felt at the next general election where the coalition lost to the Conservatives.

But none of this endless talking dealt with the real issue, which was what message did the treatment of Indians by the British on that day, and the subsequent lack of formal punishment, send out to the people of India? The answer is that this incident would galvanise the Indian nationalist movement, change the focus of many national leaders and ultimately lead to independence for both India and Pakistan. It also enables a frank examination of the reality of the British Raj, and leads us to ask, one hundred years on, are we ready to acknowledge the mistakes of the past and make amends with an official apology? This dilemma has become the ultimate legacy of the Amritsar Massacre.

This book examines the history of the British in India, and the relationship the Raj held with its people before and after Amritsar. It also investigates how Reginald Dyer came to believe he could dispatch civilians by force, regardless of their level of involvement in political agitation. The book discusses the events in the run up to the shooting, the massacre itself and the aftermath – both immediately and in the longer term. From here it shows how the events at the Jallianwala Bagh gave Indian nationalism and its leaders the push they needed to secure a free India, and in turn create the separate Muslim state of Pakistan. Finally, it looks at the modern take on the event and the call for an official apology in its centenary year.

Chapter 1

The Origins of the British in India

Many of the issues surrounding the Amritsar Massacre are connected with British influence on, and ultimately the British rule of, India. And, as a topic, it is as highly complex and controversial today as it was at the time of the mass shooting that continues to cast a shadow over memories of the British Empire. In fact, it is impossible to discuss the rationale behind the calls for home rule and nationalism in the Punjab in 1919 – and the forces that were so determined to ignore them – without first considering exactly what both sides of the debate had to gain – and perhaps more importantly to lose – if the governance of the country had changed hands.

But exactly why were the British in charge in India, a country so much larger than itself and so far away from home? How did the British army (rather than the civil service and government) end up managing so much of civilian life and in this case concerns over disturbances and unrest? And how did the British justify their presence in India and the autocratic way in which they chose to govern? The short answer is, it's a long story. And like most stories, it includes the desire to create and retain wealth and power by both groups and individuals, some good fortune along that journey and plenty of mismanagement. It starts with the desire to possess what belongs to someone else.

While colonialism has been going on ever since man could walk from his cave to that of his neighbour, it wasn't until European explorers landed in India in the late 1400s that the benefits of trading became a possibility for the continent as a whole. Spain, Portugal and the Netherlands were all interested in these faraway lands and the potential riches they offered. It was no different in Britain, and during the Renaissance period, under the reign of Henry VIII, interest in India grew, with the British Jesuit Thomas Stevens arriving in Goa in 1579. As this demonstrates, not

1

all the opportunities overseas offered material gains; much of early colonisation was designed more to spread religious beliefs and thus potentially earn something far more valuable than worldly goods – a sense of righteousness! The Portuguese were particularly fervent in their desire to bring Catholicism to the masses for example. It didn't win them many friends, and ironically opened the doors to the British.

Of course, the majority of trips were made with purely earthly benefits in mind. In 1583, a group of London merchants sailed to North Africa and then travelled 3,000 miles overland to reach India. This was at a time when lack of refrigeration made spices essential for preserving meat and disguising the taste of food that was past its best. The finest of those spices came from islands such as Java and Sumatra and India was a possible route to that bounty. Trading directly with these lands would also offer Europeans a chance to cut costs incurred by import and export taxes raised by other sellers.

Unfortunately, the Dutch already controlled the Spice Islands of the Indies, and they weren't keen on sharing with the British merchants, causing constant friction. Eventually, the Massacre of Amboyna saw Dutch supremacy and the British instead decided to focus their efforts on India, which – in time – became quite the consolation prize. While the Portuguese had claimed some of India for themselves, they had been aggressive in their acquisition and over-zealous with their religion, so the natives were more welcoming to these newer British traders. It's possible that they, or their ancestors, may have come to have regret that hospitality.

By 31 December 1600, the group of merchants saw their enterprise - The East India Trading Company – incorporated by royal charter and the foundations of British India were unwittingly laid. The ruling Mughal Emperor Jahangir was impressed by the naval prowess and business approach of the British and so allowed them to trade and build factories in India to facilitate commerce. Under the 1612 accord, the British secured the right to trade in return for protection against other imperialists. Little did India understand how in time, it might need protection from its new ally.

The East India Company grew rich and powerful from its trade in items such as cotton, silk, indigo, saltpetre, opium and spice, with India made up of many areas – each controlled by a wealthy ruler – rather than the one large country we now know it as. Increasingly however, for the Company to remain profitable it needed to establish more control over anyone at home or abroad that threatened its trade routes or commercial stability. Luckily for the Company, Cromwell introduced the Navigation Act, and all colonial trade had to be carried by British ships, that were also afforded protection by the British Navy. Cromwell also gave the traders a helping hand with his aggressive policy against the Netherlands, reducing the effectiveness of the Dutch navy. Fortune favours the brave – but it also favours the biggest and boldest in the battle too.

By the mid-1740s, the East India Company was facing rivalry from both European trading companies and local rulers, but Britain established military supremacy by 1756, as the victor in the Seven Years War against France and Spain, which proved to be the conclusive conflict in the tussle for territories. Robert Clive, twice Governor of Bengal, was at the helm during the Battle of Plassey in 1757, which crushed the French and their Indian allies, bringing Bengal under the control of the Company too. The win established Britain as the principal power. Britain was increasing its supremacy in India and in some ways also its dependency on the income from its ever-increasing territory.

By 1765, the Company was also harvesting the revenues of Bengal, Bihar and Orissa on the say-so of the Mughal Emperor. Slowly but surely the East India Company acquired more territories using its own private army (which by 1803 was twice the size of the British army), taking over areas by force and often offering local rulers the chance to keep some of their wealth and status if they acted as puppet sovereigns at the expense of the people that lived in the area. The self-interested local leaders were happy to step aside to the heavily-armed invaders if it meant not only keeping their heads, but also their riches and titles.

Expansion continued and when a cash-strapped Charles II married the Portuguese Princess Catherine of Braganza he rented out Bombay (which came as part of Catherine's dowry) to the Company. The traders were also able to establish Fort St William in Calcutta, which soon became an important and prosperous town. The Company successfully established three large areas of British power on the West and South East coasts and on the Ganges Delta. It wasn't always easy however. At times, business was threatened by the decline of the Moghul Empire and even a rival British trading company. And it also became clear that exporting to India from Britain was not always profitable – as the goods were often unsuited to life in the tropics and far too expensive for the natives to buy. Much later, some might argue that the future British success lay in damaging beyond repair the native industries in the colonies so that British exports would become a necessity. More British goods would also be needed as more of British society moved to India as it was determined to replicate its lifestyle, however unsuited it proved to be.

Ultimately, any wealth that those lands brought with them, and any income made, passed into Company coffers and in turn back to Britain via tax, trade or personal wealth. With its vast revenues and administrative control, the company changed from being merely a highly-successful trader to an omnipotent sovereign. And any political and regulatory decisions made were always designed to favour the increasing wealth and control of the Company and its shareholders, many of whom were also sitting in the British parliament making the laws that governed colonial trade and behaviour.

The East India Company was the dominant power in the subcontinent, and because of that, Britain's supremacy remained undisputed. However, as the saying goes 'power corrupts and absolute power corrupts absolutely', and there were growing concerns about mismanagement at the Company. By 1773, the Regulating Act began to exert some government control over the East India Company. With closer scrutiny, the morals of those in charge in India were questioned. Warren Hastings – the Governor from 1773 to 1785 – faced charges of corruption three years after returning home from his post. He was acquitted but ruined and cases like his raised ethical questions about the Company's role in India, whether a commercial company should shape society and if the British government had a moral responsibility for its Indian subjects. Clearly this last question is still relevant to the discussions about Amritsar today.

But legislating for India was difficult. When parliament made a bid for greater control in India via a bill introduced by the Fox-North government, it was rejected in the House of Lords, partly because George III was openly against it. The coalition government collapsed, ushering in the new government of William Pitt the Younger. The Prime Minister managed to get the India Act of 1784 passed, giving the British parliament a supervisory role in administrative and political affairs of the country. By 1833, the Charter Act was scaling down commercial operations even more, so that a year later, the Company was little more than a managing agency for the British government of India. Effectively the Company had established a trading empire through, often questionable, force and had now handed over the control of that empire to the British government. But there were still more changes to come.

Dual control of India between traders and statesmen became an uneasy mishmash of laws and morality – with conflicting beliefs and politics and a widening gap between the wealthy and the poor. Life as an expat could be boring, soldiers and civil servants both worked long hours in a climate they weren't accustomed to, usually having left their family behind. Drinking and gambling were common, as were inter-racial relationships. Despite these problems however, there's no denying that the military success of the East India Company helped establish more and more British territory to rule over. Between 1824 and 1856, the necessity of ensuring the continued commercial success of the Company meant that wars were fought and eventually won in Burma, Sind, the Punjab, Nagpur, Avadh and Afghanistan. While many of the wars were often not strategically well planned, they served one goal – to keep the Company profitable, removing anyone or anything that threatened that. By 1856, seventy per cent of the subcontinent was British controlled.

Perhaps because much of the land grab was more about seizing a commercial opportunity than building an empire to govern, the arrangements that followed the annexation of an area were varied. In many cases, a local Prince was allowed to continue to rule on British terms – keeping his wealth, privilege, status, lifestyle and property – and saving the invaders the chore and cost of setting up a local government. However, the native ruler had little say in administration, with each significant Indian principality also under the auspices of a British administrator. Thus, many of the governing decisions were designed to favour nothing other than the Company's business and certainly did not pause to consider native interests, an example perhaps, that continued to be followed even if more discreetly. The Company's work became increasingly about admin and taxation and provided jobs for many British expats. As more British workers set up home in India for the long term, Indian and Europeans began to mix less and less – it became more common for families to move out to India, and with British women now in the subcontinent, romantic liaisons with natives also fell from favour. A divide began to open up, and it would continue to widen as social and political life added more and more divisions.

For the first time, the question of how to rule Indian natives became an issue – and this is where relations between rulers and the ruled became even more strained. The Company – clearly missing a sense of irony – decided that the moral welfare of its subjects was its responsibility. It set about making some Indian customs illegal – not in itself a bad thing when those customs involved '*suttee*' or '*sati*', the 'voluntary' burning of a Hindi widow on her husband's funeral pyre, and female infanticide – where female newborns were killed because of the financial burden that a wedding dowry would bring to her parents. However, having had missionary work and education already over-zealously bestowed upon them, the natives began to resent implications that their culture was in need of changing. And, indeed, the Company and some of its British employees were far from paragons of virtue.

Another sticking point was the development of road and railway systems designed to make trade and communication far easier for the Company but which actually posed problems for those following a caste system because of a far greater potential for overcrowding and ritual pollution. Even within the military, the demand for troops to cross the sea could result in a loss of caste for Hindi soldiers. And perhaps they noticed that when their traditions, such as the 'doctrine of lapse', which allowed a land grab when there was no relation to inherit a principality as used by Governor General Lord Dalhousie, were accepted as and when it suited the British, they felt just a little conned. For many, Britain had dispossessed landlords, overthrown local rulers, banned Indian traditions and attacked the cultural and religious order that formed their way of life. And for some, this lack of sensitivity had gone to far. Trouble was brewing, but the blinkered British businessmen were too busy counting cash to notice.

Typically, the Company's still large and effective army was made up of sepoys or Indian soldiers. These soldiers were issued with new Enfield P-53 rifles which used cartridges that required greasing to load. In an astonishing lack of cultural sensitivity, and in a move that would herald its further demise, the Company issued the sepoys, who were mostly Hindu and Muslim, with grease for the rifles made from the fat of cows and pigs – animals that for religious reasons they could not touch. As a result of this and other grievances, a mutiny of sepoys of the Company's army in the garrison town of Meerut began on 10 May 1857. Again, without forethought, dissenters were dealt with harshly and

85 sepoys were sentenced to hard labour and paraded in disgrace. Other discontented soldiers rose up, releasing prisoners, burning property, killing Europeans and marching to Delhi. And, since timing is everything in history, if not in life, the uprising happened just as many British troops were returning from war in Persia, leaving strategic points and arms and munitions vulnerable. A civilian rebellion soon followed; fed by the resentment over social reforms, land taxes, the treatment of landowners and princes and a general dissatisfaction about how the British were managing India.

The Mutiny – although ultimately unsuccessful – worried the British authorities. The spread from barracks to back roads threatened the continued way of life in India. The massacre of females and children at Kanpur (often called Cawnpore), with rumoured sexual offences, caused fear and panic among Brits both living in the colony and back at home. The violence was aptly described as 'butchery' with two Muslim brothers who worked within the meat trade part of the group sent to kill the remaining prisoners held at Kanpur, and it would scar India forever. Accordingly, the British chose to come down hard on the mutineers as they regained control – many were shot, bayoneted or hanged. Other grim punishments included being tied across the mouth of a cannon that was then fired, or hanged inside the skin of a pig or cow to further insult the religion of the rebel. These were savage times.

The period marked a new low for Anglo-Indian relations and couldn't be reconciled with the Victorian ethos of progress that England upheld. Much was done to discredit those involved in the unrest – and natives in general. It was also widely believed – but not proven – that the first sepoy to mutiny, Mangal Pandey, was a drug user. The uprising was known as the Indian Mutiny, although strictly speaking, since civilians were also involved, it was something more. The way the Mutiny was handled and later categorized was significant as it widened the gulf between the British and Indians forever, reinforcing prejudices and making for a bitter relationship. The smouldering resentments and distrust on both sides of the battle were to resurface again and again in the lead up to the events in Amritsar in 1919 – and probably were behind the way in which Dyer handled native 'rebellion'.

A year after this period of unrest, the Company itself became its main casualty; the Government of India Act was passed and full control was officially transferred from the Company to the India Office, a government department. By 1874, the East India Company was officially dissolved, and shareholders were financially compensated. The Company had effectively ruled India from 1757 to 1858, but its mismanagement led to the British Crown assuming governmental control and absorbing its armies, effectively restructuring the relationship between England and India. Now authority came all the way from London – 5,000 miles away! Queen Victoria's British Raj was born.

Chapter 2

The Raj and its Refusal to Change

From 1858, the Crown ruled India, with the position of Governor General re-named the Viceroy and Governor General. The Viceroy also had an Executive Council to consult with, consisting of five members who each took charge of a separate department: home, revenue, military, law and finance. Located in England, the role of Secretary of State for India was established to take charge of the Viceroy. The Secretary of State for India, the political head of the India Office, was responsible to Parliament and had a fifteen-man council of advisors, known as the Council of India. It wasn't an easy arrangement for many reasons. To begin with, the advisors were often ex-Company themselves and so any changes tended to be conservative. The other MPs in England also knew little about the colony – and often weren't interested either, with the annual debate on the India budget notoriously poorly attended. There was also a time difference, the distant geographical location and lack of reliable communications to contend with (the telegraph was only invented in 1880s) as the Secretary of State tried to control his charge from his new office in Whitehall.

Other organisational changes included legislative control being transferred to local councils for Bengal, the Punjab and the North West Provinces. The army was restructured and controlled by the state, with Indian soldiers no longer allowed to handle artillery for fear that, if equipped, they may rise up again and use their arms against their rulers. Attempts were instead made to beef up the number of British soldiers in the army, but when this proved problematic the numbers of Sikhs, Gurkhas and those from the tribes in the North West were ramped up instead. These races were thought to be more likely to stick with the British if they suppressed the Hindi or Muslim civilians from other parts of the country. The loyal Indian Princes also did well out of the new arrangements, retaining their status if not any actual power.

And the changes led to a revival of conservative Hinduism as a knee-jerk reaction to the perceived threat of British influence on their traditions. Indeed, for the next half century, conservatism was the preferred option for both Englishman and Indian.

After the uprising in 1857, India was in some ways easier to govern. Out of Company control, the British Government could put in place their own policies and standards and an efficient and fair civil service was established, although some may argue that the civil service was far more 'fair' if you were a British white man seeking your fortune in India, rather than an educated Indian looking for advancement. The Viceroy – typically in place for about five years - presided over Governors of the larger provinces and they in turn over civil servants and those enforcing regulations and laws. However, the rift between Europeans and Indians continued to widen; the British were often fearful of more trouble and in an effort to show they were still in charge there was always plenty of pomp surrounding British dignitaries and events.

Typically, the Viceroy was a politician who had never reached his full potential or who was past his best. More ambitious and hopeful ministers stayed close to London, to make sure they were considered for Prime Minister if the call came. Although the role of Viceroy might not have been the choice of those with a glittering political career ahead of them, it was an incredibly powerful position. By 1901, India's Viceroy presided over three hundred million subjects and commanded one the finest armies in the world. That was an incredible privilege to have on your CV – and many were Earls, Viscounts and Marquises. But, without too many political ambitions himself, the Viceroy was not usually intent on making waves but rather in keeping the status quo and enjoying an easy life (a rather splendid easy life!). It was probably believed that a period of stability and conservatism was what was needed to prevent further unrest. Two Viceroys bucked the trend however, attempting to pass reforms during their tenure. The first was Lord Ripon, during his appointment by the Liberal government in 1880 to 1884, and the second was Lord Curzon, who was Viceroy from 1898 to 1905 under a Unionist-Conservative government.

India became incredibly important during the Victorian era for both economic reasons and the status it brought Britain. Nineteen per cent of British exports arrived there, with hundreds of millions of pounds invested in the subcontinent. And, perhaps most importantly, the cost of

running India, its civil service and its army was borne by the natives –
who, through the taxes they were required to pay, effectively financed their
own subjection, a point not lost on modern historians and commentators.
When Queen Victoria was proclaimed the Empress of India in 1877,
many thought it was a shrewd move by Conservative Prime Minister
Benjamin Disraeli, designed perhaps to encourage loyalty from Indian
Princes that ruled much of the territory. The celebrations surrounding her
appointment were another symbolic attempt at showing the splendour
of the British troops and administration. The queen herself never visited
India of course (or any of her major colonies for that matter), although
she was particularly fond of her Indian servant Abdul Karim, who was a
'gift from India', designed to help Victoria address the Indian princes at
her lavish golden Jubilee banquet. The relationship between the queen and
her '*munshi*' – or teacher – was to become an intense one, although after
years of favouritism by the queen, Karim was unceremoniously sacked by
Edward VII just a few hours after Victoria's funeral.

The British government had plenty of ideas on how they wanted to
run India – as well as enforcing law and order, the Raj wanted to improve
education, health, irrigation and agriculture and control famine. These
were massive tasks – and progress was often slow – as it was back home
in Britain and elsewhere in the world at that time. The Victorian concept
of charity was also rather harsh and hinged on the idea that too much
help was a bad thing, with those on the receiving end likely to become
less self-reliant. Under British rule, industry did develop, and by 1914,
India was among the top fourteen most industrialised nations. Again,
the usefulness of this for the natives remains debatable. It could also be
claimed (and disputed) that the Raj made some improvements in legal,
economic and educational fields during the fifty or so years after the
Mutiny. Many British considered this progress as a noble mission of
ruling a lesser people for their own good, overlooking that this noble
mission was also rather financially favourable for the British too…

But the lack of long-term planning by the British saw the growth of
a wealthier, healthier and better-educated section of society that then
experienced frustration with the lack of respect and self-governance
it was shown and allowed. While the poor were too busy surviving to
consider rebellion, during the late Victorian era a new class of so-called
'*babus*' emerged. While *babu* was originally a term showing respect or
endearment, the British in India used the term pejoratively, usually to

refer to Indian clerks or other civil servants. These men were the product of the British education system in India, often having graduated from Calcutta or Bombay University. While on paper they were qualified for many roles in the Civil Service, they were still not actually accepted and it was well known Eton- and Oxford-educated Viceroy Curzon did not consider Indians suitable for government. And despite Liberal thinkers like William Gladstone suggesting India must be run for Indians, many of those already enjoying the elevated status and high-salary of the establishment, saw any advancement of the natives as a threat. The Europeans truly believed that they were superior to the indigenous people. It was an attitude that permeated every decision made – and the attitude that would ultimately allow the events in Amritsar to unfold.

The response to the proposed Ilbert Bill of 1883, introduced during the Viceroyalty of the Liberal Marquess of Ripon, George Robinson, was a prime example of the prejudices held by the British. The bill – which was dubbed 'the white mutiny' by its many detractors – mooted the idea that Indians with the appropriate magistrate qualifications should be allowed to practice and therefore try Europeans brought before them. The Bill was not well received and led to intense opposition in both Britain and India and was eventually revised before it was enacted in 1884 to ensure that only an all-white jury could try a European. This move suggests that for some, even a white criminal was somehow superior to an educated and professional Indian.

But by the turn of the century things were changing in India – just as they were changing across the world. Global events like the First World War saw many changes and back in Britain, 1905 saw a Liberal government voted in. In the same year Viceroy Curzon resigned – his reforms had brought conflict and controversy and clashes with Arthur James Balfour's Unionist Conservative government. Curzon for example was keen to have the border states of Afghanistan and Tibet brought under his control but that could have brought conflict with Russia, not something the government back home wanted to risk. Curzon also clashed with Indian commander in chief, Field Marshal Kitchener, who controlled military and defence spending, and squabbled with many senior civil servants and army commanders. As a result, those Curzon had upset knocked back many of the reforms he wanted, despite the positive outcomes they may have brought and when he offered his resignation it was happily accepted.

One change Curzon did manage to make however was to have a lasting effect – and a negative one at that. Curzon sanctioned the partition of Bengal in July 1905, designed to make administration easier. Unfortunately, it upset the people of Bengal, who were typically well educated and politically aware. The move encouraged nationalism and the Indian National Congress – originally little more than a middle-class talking shop when formed in 1885 – rose up behind the cause. The Muslim League, founded in 1906, also voiced nationalist views.

Previously, Bengal, Bihar, and Orissa had formed a single province of British India since 1765 but, as it had grown, it became too large for a single administration. Curzon decided to unite Assam with fifteen districts of east Bengal to create a new province with a mainly Muslim population of thirty-one million and a capital at Dacca (now Dhaka in Bangladesh). This threatened the Hindus in West Bengal, who were typically in charge of the commercial, professional and rural life, who complained that if Bengal were split in two, they would become a minority in this newly created province. For the Hindus, it reeked of an attempt to stamp out the developed Bengali nationalism and there was agitation including mass meetings and a national boycott of British goods. While the agitation was suppressed and the partition went ahead, it allowed an underground terrorist movement to form that would later return. Eventually, the Bengal partition would be reversed in an attempt at appeasement but conversely that damaged relations with those the move had favoured, in this case Bengali Muslims. It really was an exercise in what not to do and not the first or last time decisions were made for the wrong reasons with undesirable effects.

The British could still count on the support of the princes however – and the landlord class – both of whom had too much to lose if the current system that they had done so well out of collapsed. Their wealth and status was too precious to risk, and it could be argued that supporting a class system in India helped to maintain British rule; vested interests are an incredibly powerful force. There was also support from some sections of society that had fared well in industry – such as the Tata family, who were pioneers in Indian industrialism and went on to own cotton mills, iron and steel works and hydroelectric power plants. The very poor that led a hand to mouth existence were not in any position to rebel of course. They would need a uniting force to enable them to realize the power of the masses – it would come later in the guise of Gandhi.

In Britain, the Liberal Government introduced the Indian Councils Act of 1909, which became known as the Morley-Minto Reforms after the Secretary of State for India John Morley and the Viceroy Lord Minto. These were designed to introduce more elected and nominated Indians to the provincial and central legislative councils of the Raj as a response to the call by educated Indians for a greater say in the way the country was run. The move suggested that the authorities were prepared to move towards Indian self-governance, but it's more likely that it was something of a confidence trick, with the reforms designed to save the British Raj from being challenged by the middle classes and to keep them on side as nationalism grew in popularity. Many of the concessions at the time sounded strong on paper, but in practice offered little change – the Indian Civil Service for example, was in theory open to natives, except that the entrance exams were held in the UK. It must have been particularly frustrating to take up the educational opportunities offered but to be then denied access to the professional positions that would allow you to use them. The Morley-Minto reforms were not received well at home however, nor welcomed by the British in India. The press, the Conservative party, Edward VII and George, Prince of Wales, were all known to be against them. Reform – and respect for the Indian in India – would be a long time coming.

By 1914, England found itself at war. It relied heavily on India during this period, recruiting two million soldiers, tens of thousands of whom died in the bloody battles of the European Western Front and Mesopotamia (figures put this at more than sixty-two thousand). Despite some unrest – notably the 5th Light Infantry in Singapore that mutinied and murdered several officers when it was rumoured they would be shipped off to France and when Mullahs instructed Muslim troops not to invade Turkey – Indian troops remained surprisingly loyal during the war and were, in fact, to prove invaluable. This was despite food shortages, a clampdown on civil rights and rising land prices. It is likely that many of the Indian population felt united in the desire to conquer a bigger enemy and hoped that it could trust its sovereign to fulfill the implicitly suggested move to political change in the subcontinent in the future. It proved to be false hope however.

As a reward for loyalty during the war, India found itself being treated as an equal to other important imperial nations – such as Australia, Canada, New Zealand and South Africa – when it was invited to the

Imperial War Conference of 1917. The meeting was held alongside the Imperial War Cabinet, the British Empire's wartime coordinating body, to plan governance of the British Empire during the war and prepare for post-war politics. Through the invite, Prime Minister Lloyd George acknowledged the importance of India to the war effort. In the same year, the Indian Secretary for State, Edwin Montagu, visited for talks regarding the future of British rule in India. Montagu supported a further round of reforms in India, based on the success that the Councils Act had had with alienating more extremist views on independence, and allowing Indians a bigger role in local and provincial government, while still keeping central British rule. Montagu wanted to go a step further and made a declaration that Britain's ultimate goal was Indian self-government – albeit achieved by a gradual process and with India remaining part of the Empire.

Cynics have suggested that the promise of Home Rule for India was simply a canny way of ensuring India remained loyal in turbulent times. Further down the line, Montagu, who supported social reform generally, found himself urging the Indian government to be moderate when responding to protests; it was he who wanted a stronger condemnation of General Dyer for Amritsar, even though he didn't perhaps push hard enough to get one. He also warned the government not to provoke Indian Muslim opinion by partitioning Turkey, the only Muslim power and seat of the Caliphate. This view brought him into conflict with Lloyd George and led to his resignation and ultimately the loss of his seat in parliament. Nationalists, however, grew impatient with promises of more independence at a future date and they found new hope in the return to India of British-educated barrister Mohandas Karamchand Gandhi in 1915. Gandhi was well known for mobilizing Indian political action against the white supremacist regime in South Africa – using his non-violent technique of *satyagraha* or 'strength of truth'. This approach, that hoped to win struggles through the use of example, restraint and superior moral character, was hailed as the one that could finally empower the Indian masses in the struggle for independence. Certainly, the Indian population could not have beaten British rule by entering into a war, and any successful approach would have to be accessible to all levels of society.

In 1917, the *satyagraha* method was put to its first Indian test – in Champaran, Bihar – when European planters tried to turn the price rise of indigo to their advantage. Natives had been obliged by their European landlords to cultivate indigo on a portion of their land (15 per cent) in return for nominal compensation under the *tinkathia* system, but as market competition made it no longer profitable, landlords looked to increase rents and tax in exchange for the release from the obligation. Gandhi took up the cause and forced the authorities to abandon their plans. The *tinkathia* system was abolished and the workers were financially compensated; within a decade, the European planters left the area. A year later, Gandhi was integral in the Ahmedabad Mill Strike, which was a reaction to a pay dispute between the mill owners and labourers. In support of his call for a thirty-five per cent wage rise, Gandhi went on a hunger strike and the mill owners eventually agreed to go to tribunal. The pay increase was awarded to the workers. In 1918, Gandhi also organised a *satyagraha* in Kheda in Gujarat, where crops were less than a quarter of the normal yield. The workers appealed for remission of the land revenue, to which they were entitled, but the government had ignored the plea. The government relented and issued instructions that revenue should be recovered only from those that could afford to pay. The new approach was working and the British would have been wise to see this as an indication that India and her people were changing.

It was Gandhi's return to his homeland that helped usher in the new – and ultimately successful – era of nationalist activism. He was completely different from the rest of the Indian elite, who had appropriated the Western way of life from the Raj and who were unable to inspire the masses. Instead, Gandhi had spent two decades in South Africa perfecting his political and personal philosophy and by this time was opposed to the education system and scientific techniques touted by foreigners. He advocated and promoted cottage industries and supported religious retreat. His approach of passive civil disobedience and non-violent confrontation became the ultimate weapon in the battle for independence, partly because it did not fight the Raj with physical might and also because it was easy to follow, allowing ordinary Indians to take up the cause and the strength in numbers was something the Raj could never match. Gandhi's self-confidence and charisma plus his rejection of Western culture and business helped stop the Indian people feeling inferior to their rulers. He became the natural leader for a movement that was no longer prepared to accept top-down rule.

With a new-found resolve, by the end of the First World War, the Indian people were a changed population. Unfortunately, the Raj administration seriously underestimated the change in public opinion and – perhaps foolishly – proposed two Acts in 1919 that attempted to continue the restrictions on civil liberties they'd felt necessary to impose during the war. The Acts were named after a British judge, Sir Sidney Rowlatt who oversaw the committee that decided measures such as indefinite detention and incarceration without trial were necessary after the war. The Acts also allowed for tight restrictions on the press, juryless trials carried out in secret and measures that made it easier to arrest and imprison those suspected of terrorism. The bills, which when passed as just one Act, became the Anarchical and Revolutionary Crimes Act of 1919, banned free speech and the right to assembly and were in conflict with the promise of responsible government the Montagu Declaration had offered just two years earlier.

It was the audacity of this about face that ultimately set in motion the events of the Amritsar Massacre and the brutal martial law imposed for several months afterwards. Nationalists were further outraged when Dyer was only punished minimally by the authorities, even being celebrated in some corners of the establishment.

Chapter 3

British India after Amritsar

From the Amritsar Massacre, it was a downwards spiral for the Raj. The events in Amritsar and its aftermath coupled with the Rowlatt Acts were the reason the idea of Home Rule was no longer acceptable to Gandhi and other nationalists, and even British politicians began to accept they needed to hand over the reins. Thus, the inter-war period saw many reforms and concessions designed to slowly bring about devolution. For Britain however, India still held enormous economic value and symbolic significance. It's often suggested that the many negotiations and changes in policy that took place at this time were simply delaying tactics to put off the inevitable loss of the colony.

The 1919 Government of India Act, which received royal assent in December that year, was one such move that seemed at first glance to encourage more Indian involvement in government, as it enlarged the Indian electorate and provided a dual form of government for the major provinces. However, under closer inspection, while British and Indian ministers shared office, the Indian ministers were in charge of areas such as education, health, agriculture and irrigation while Brits were in charge of the justice system, the police and revenue – the areas that wielded the most control. And above all this, the Viceroy could still veto any new laws he wasn't happy with, suspend councils that misbehaved and use the armed forces as he wished.

As well as using the one step forward, two steps back approach, the British have also been accused of creating new systems that worked against independence by using reforms to further tie India's elite and educated into a British system, making change less appealing for them. The British are also accused of encouraging divisions in Indian society both via offering new positions of power to limited numbers and by separating citizens into religious groups, for example by introducing a separate Muslim electoral roll. Further separatism occurred when the British decided that Gandhi, who was a Hindu, and his Congress party, were worth working with. Rival Muslim politicians in the Muslim League feared this relationship would lead to a Hindu-dominated government, and this unease led to other unfortunate decisions and alliances further down the line. Despite these machinations, in the 1920s, some progress was made in 'Indianising' both the civil service and army, and applications from British citizens fell dramatically, sending the message that the British in England knew India was no longer the prospect it had once been.

While some opposition continued from the British, particularly those like Lord Birkenhead, a British Conservative politician and barrister, who served as Secretary of State for India between 1924 and 1928, and who still considered Indians uncivilized and incapable of self-government, by 1929, the Labour minority government released a clear statement that constitutional freedom for India was on the cards. This Irwin Declaration – named after the Viceroy at the time – still however meant that India would attain just Dominion status, self-governing within the Empire-Commonwealth. The first of several Round Table Conferences involving British India was also chaired, discussing constitutional progress. These meetings eventually led to the 1935 Government of India Act, which seemed to guarantee India's independence via a Home Rule agreement. However, before that could be seen through, war broke out and Britain instead turned its attentions to Nazi Germany and its associates in Italy. India was vitally important to the war, because of the manpower it could offer, its first-rate army, air force and naval bases and also because of where it lay geographically. This was no time to hand it more power.

The decision to involve India in the Second World War – or rather the way it was announced - led to problems that would have long-lasting implications for a unified India. The autocratic Viceroy Lord Linlithgow took it upon himself to declare publicly that India was at war without any consultation or democratic process. The insensitive and high-handed approach only served to alienate Congress, who opposed fascism but expected to be treated more equally in the decision to stand with Britain and would – quite reasonably – have anticipated also being involved in the announcement of the decision. Consequently, the ministries in the provinces run by Congress resigned in protest, effectively handing control back to the Civil Service and British hands. The Muslim League used this split to co-operate with the British, seizing the opportunity to be the 'favourite child'.

By 1941, and the attack on Pearl Harbor, the nationalists were happy to work with Britain against the mutual enemy. As the war progressed however, Nehru and Congress leaders used the co-operative times to ask for a statement that after the war India would be free to determine its own destiny. The British government chose to pass on this crucial opportunity to work with Congress however, and Viceroy Lord Willingdon even went as far as to ban discussion on constitutional issues. As the Japanese drew ever closer to India, though, the situation changed. British, Dutch and French empires fell – and Singapore surrendered, Japanese forces were soon in Burma and began bombing Calcutta and other cities. India needed security so Prime Minister Winston Churchill sent Sir Stafford Cripps to the subcontinent in 1942 to appease its wartime ally America, and to offer Indian nationalists post war independence. The Cripps Mission proposed immediate inclusion of Indian leaders in the government of India and allowed provinces with a Muslim majority to opt out.

But Gandhi was convinced he could beat the Japanese without cosying up to the British. Congress rejected the proposals and instead passed its 'Quit India' resolution that called for immediate dismantling of the Raj. In response, British authorities arrested hundreds of Congress leaders and violent protests broke out across the territory. The Raj restored order using the armed forces and the police. An unfortunate by-product of the somewhat shortsighted move to lock up many of the leaders within Congress was the void it left behind. The Muslim League moved quickly to fill that space. Its leader, Muhammad Ali Jinnah, launched a new resolution telling the British to 'Divide and Quit'. While the British ignored the resolution, they did begin to co-operate with the Muslim League, subsiding its newspaper via advertising. This new relationship was to eventually lead to Partition. Building on the fear that the Raj would simply be replaced by a Hindu government, the League grew in numbers and support increased for the demand for a separate Muslim homeland – Pakistan.

As the war continued, Subhas Chandra Bose from the Congress party formed the Indian National Army, looking for backing from the Japanese and Germans and recruiting those kept in Japanese prisoner of war camps. He hoped for a military uprising that would finally topple the Raj, but his hopes were to be dashed as the allies regained control of Asia, reclaiming Burma, Malaya, Borneo and Hong Kong. After the war, the INA volunteers had to be punished for their treason, although the Raj chose to tread lightly with a symbolic move, charging just one Hindu, one Muslim and one Sikh and pardoning them. They also destroyed the INA memorial in Singapore.

By the end of the war, the Raj was still in place although it received no support in rebuilding the Empire from its former allies the USA and Russia. In summer 1945, the general election in Britain saw a landslide victory for Labour, a party that typically supported Indian independence. Unbelievably, India still had to wait another two years to be free of its imperial masters. The new Attlee government was incredibly cautious in its approach to handing back power and relations continued to be strained. The British government also prioritized its own affairs as it worked to create the Welfare State and push the policy of nationalisation at home, rather than tackle the India issue. As it waited, India held its own elections – this time the Muslim League were far stronger, although Congress remained popular with voters too. This led to more demands for a separate state. Mutinies by British RAF servicemen waiting to go home, by the Indian Air Force and by the navies in Bombay, Calcutta, Madras and Karachi added pressure to the situation and Attlee finally sent a delegation to India to hammer out a deal.

Unfortunately, Congress and the Muslim League could not find common ground over the establishment of Pakistan, despite the British suggesting a Union government. The situation became more complex and confused and even an interim government could not be agreed upon by the League's Jinnah and Nehru from Congress. Instead, the League held a day of Direct Action on 16 August 1946, which saw violent rioting, leading to many deaths, especially in Calcutta. For Dyer's supporters this proved that he was right to try to spare bloodshed.

Amid this confusion, Congress pushed on with the idea of an interim government, outlining fifteen members, made up of five caste Hindus, five Muslims, one scheduled caste and four minority representatives. The Viceroy announced the ministers and, rather than be left out, Jinnah eventually agreed to join. Finally, an accord seemed to have been achieved, although ultimately it failed too, and any new constitution seemed doomed. More rioting broke out and spread across North India. Eventually, the Prime Minister could take no more and announced a deadline of June for British withdrawal from India. A new Viceroy – Earl Mountbatten of Burma - was announced and sworn in on 24 March.

Mountbatten made a decisive Viceroy, was of royal blood and knowledgeable about Asia. Both he and Lady Mountbatten were Labour sympathisers and in favour of colonial freedom. They were also on friendly terms with Nehru. This friendship led Mountbatten to reveal his plans for the future of India to Nehru at a social event in Simla. The plans centred around 'Plan Balkan', which devolved power to each province, who could then negotiate with central government to form a union. Nehru was horrified at the idea as it left India open to become a mass of separate states and shared his concerns with the new viceroy. While Mountbatten had planned to reveal his idea at a meeting with nationalists scheduled for 17 May, he instead cancelled the meeting to give himself time to re-jig his proposals, only allowing a split from the central government if a majority of voters in a province agreed to it. The plans also allowed for partitioning and redrawing of the boundaries of Bengal and the Punjab and proposed a referendum for the North West Frontier Province. But, aware that Nehru had had a preview of the plans, the League were not happy and went on to refuse to let Mountbatten become the first Governor of Pakistan, despite the newly independent India being happy to agree to the idea.

As the bureaucrats continued making plans for the new constitution, violence spread across Lahore and Calcutta, and it became clear that the only thing that would stop the outbursts was for the British to hand over. Mountbatten insisted that India accept Dominion status and stay in the Commonwealth, and to speed up the process it was agreed. By early June 1947, the Viceroy, followed by Nehru, Jinnah and Sikh Baldev Singh were able to broadcast their agreement to the nation. The transfer date was set for 15 August and it became a reality at midnight on that date. Nehru became the Prime Minister of India. The creation of the new state of Pakistan had come the day before.

Unfortunately, the handover did not run smoothly, millions migrated to their chosen state amid violence and mass killings and it was the same story as Bengal was divided too. It's likely a million Indians died in the period, putting the bloodshed at Amritsar into perspective for some. Gandhi resorted to fasting in an attempt to convince Hindus and Muslims to live peacefully together, but his views upset extremists and he was assassinated on 30 January the next year. Amritsar – and perhaps more so the handling of it – proved to be the catalyst that nationalism needed to make Indian independence a reality. Unfortunately, the political struggles between the main players combined with a world war and the legacy of divide and conquer meant the path was not a smooth one. There had been further bloodshed after Amritsar, ultimately Dyer's bold claims he had prevented it were proved wrong.

Chapter 4

Reginald Dyer: Man, Monster, Myth

With the bare facts of the events of 13 April 1919 before us, General Reginald Dyer sounds like a monster. He ordered his troops to fire on a crowd of unarmed, men, women and children trapped in an enclosed area, many of whom were simply in Amritsar to celebrate a religious festival. He did not ask the crowds to disperse, or give any warning that shots would be fired if they didn't, and he instructed his men to continue shooting until all their ammunition was spent, leaving just enough for protection during a swift exit. He then refused to let the wounded be helped and the dead be taken for burial until the following day by the application of a curfew. The terror and suffering of those caught up in the events cannot be underestimated, and their memories still haunt their descendants today. His actions certainly make Reginald Dyer unique – for never before or since has such violence been unleashed upon civilians by a British officer; which is why he became known as the 'Butcher of Amritsar', the soldier responsible for savage slaughter.

And yet, Dyer was also a loving husband and father, apparently popular with the soldiers in his command and with many of the ladies of the British Raj who made much effort to thank and support him after the massacre. He was also a studious and dedicated man who had fought valiantly for his country when asked – many attended his funeral. After the massacre, Dyer still had many supporters in India and in England within the army and in civilian life too. Some thought of him as a hero and the 'Saviour of India', and Dyer always maintained he had done what was necessary at the time to prevent further bloodshed in the region. How did this officer come to commit an act that had such far-reaching implications? Did he act in isolation – or did he really have the support of his superiors from the outset? Was he an embodiment of all that was wrong with Imperialism? Why did he decide that a show of extreme force was necessary and justified?

Did he ever fully understand that his actions led to a chain of events that would ultimately destroy the India he was trying to preserve? To answer these questions, we must look to the influences and experiences that shaped the man behind the massacre.

Perhaps surprisingly, for someone who seemed to hold the stereotypical British reserve and ideas of superiority over natives, Dyer was born in India in 1864. His grandfather, John Dyer had served in Bengal as a naval officer for the East India Company, moving to the subcontinent in the 1820s and only returning to England upon retirement. John Dyer had a led an exciting working life fighting piracy that was common in that area in those days, while his wife, originally from Devon, moved from England to live in India with him and bear ten children. Two of those children chose to return to India as adults – one of them was Edward Dyer, Reginald's father, who moved there originally to pursue a new life as an engineer. However, Edward's elder brother – already in the country – suggested that he instead start a brewery as British beer was in short supply and consequently over priced in the region.

The idea proved to be an exceptionally perceptive one and in 1855, fresh from a spell back home to learn the trade, Edward landed in Kasauli, where an earlier brewery had failed. His wife Mary followed a few years later just before the Mutiny in 1857. The area was a quiet one, and was not touched directly by the violence, although the Dyers heard plenty about it, as the area was a refuge for those escaping from it and was home to a sanitarium for recovering British soldiers. It's likely the family knew all about the atrocities – including those where British women and children had been targeted – such as in the events at Cawnpore. It was an unfortunate time for someone to be introduced to India, as the Mutiny left the British feeling shaken and fearful of the future. After the uprising, there was a widespread and lasting distrust of natives and the rulers and the ruled led increasingly separate lives. It is therefore possible that the Dyer children (nine in total, eventually) were aware that the adults around them felt their personal safety was at risk from Indians.

At this point in British Indian society, there seemed to be a special emphasis placed on the concern for the safety of women in India. Much has been said about the European women in the Raj being particularly anti-native, fearing for their modesty in the face of savages, although it pays to remember women were (and still are) very rarely the instigators of the values that define the accepted behaviour of their gender, their role being merely to abide by those values or attract reproach. These values clearly affected the men of Dyer's generation too and the assault on a British missionary in Amritsar a few days prior to the massacre seemed to especially shock the establishment and warrant particularly harsh reprisals.

Edward continued to have a successful career in the brewing business and was poached by a larger company, moving to Murree, set within the hills on the border of Kashmir, to manage a brewery. From there, the family moved on to Simla, to set up a new outlet. The Hill Station Simla was popular and fashionable with Europeans seeking out cooler weather in the Indian summer as Viceroy Lord Amherst started spending the hotter season there in 1827. With all these customers, the beer business was booming and the family was wealthy enough to buy a large house and garden in a desirable area and to employ servants and domestic help.

Simla continued to be a popular destination for British India, with Viceroy Sir John Lawrence establishing it as the summer capital of India, which meant that cartloads of the civil service and clerks – and their belongings – descended on the municipality as the temperature rose. It was incorporated into the Punjab in 1850 and both the army headquarters and the Government of Punjab also spent the summer there. Consequently, it also attracted quite a social scene, not least with British women seeking out an eligible bachelor to marry. With colonial picnics, garden fetes, balls, plays, hunts, cocktail parties, riding, racing and croquet the order of the day, Rudyard Kipling described the summer capital as a 'centre of power as well as pleasure'.

While the Dyer family was undoubtedly rich enough to match if not surpass these high-ranking army officers and government officials in wealth, British society in India had a rigid social hierarchy to rival Indian's own caste system, imported direct from England's upper classes. The middle-class servants of the Empire emulated the manners of the Victorian and Edwardian aristocracy in Britain and thoroughly enjoyed their elevated status. And despite having had relatives in the army and even the East India Company, the Dyers' great success in business counted against them socially – clearly marking them out as 'trade'. Being a hardworking – and successful – entrepreneur, while admirable, was not enough to grant them access to the highest society of the Raj. Instead, the Dyers would have had to be content with considering themselves superior to the Indians around them, including the brewery workers and their domestic staff. According to Dyer's biography, Dyer's father was respected in business and considered kind, although somewhat shy, possessing a reverence to women. His mother was the dominant force in the marriage – with her husband often away from home because of work – and she was stubborn with a stammer. These are the traits Reginald Dyer's parents passed down to him.

Reginald Dyer thus grew up speaking Hindustani with the native servants in his home and had an Indian nanny or '*ayah*', a common practice in British India, with most children becoming very fond of their nursemaid. He went to a local Christian school, along with other British children, typically the offspring of civil servants and the richer commercial classes. His school was closed to Indian children until 1881, reinforcing the idea that whites were superior to their Indian counterparts. As a day pupil, rather than a boarder, and coupled with his stammer, it's likely he was also somewhat of an outsider here. When not at school, he had the wilderness of Simla to enjoy, plus the hill station and its busy social scene, with plenty of shops and hotels. Sundays were spent at the Anglican Church service. It also sounds rather idyllic, not the background that would create a heartless killer.

Reginald's life changed significantly however when he was eleven. As was common for children with parents in the colonies, both he and his older brother were sent back 'home' to boarding school, and, in their case, this was to Middleton College near Cork in Ireland. Perhaps more unusual though is that they travelled to this distant and unfamiliar place alone (via train and steamer), arriving in 1875 and that Dyer stayed there for twelve years solidly. Reginald didn't see the rest of his family – or Simla – again until he was twenty-three-years-old, although he continued to learn Hindustani. Neither of his parents ever visited, even in the holidays. It's believed that the Dyer boys arrived alone wearing solar topis – sun hats – and Gurkha knives known as kukris, making them stand out upon arrival for all the wrong reasons. Looking at this situation with modern eyes, it's clear to see that being sent so far away without any idea of what would be appropriate when you got there as a young child must have had some emotional effect.

Middleton was flourishing when the Dyer boys arrived. It had a dedicated headmaster, close ties to the Church of Ireland with many masters also clergymen and pupils often went on to the top colleges at Oxford and Cambridge, and to Dublin's Trinity College and Queen's College, Belfast. The school also had an army class to prepare for a career in the forces and the option to take the Sandhurst entry exam was available. Here, in the quiet, green Irish countryside, Reginald Dyer was to change from boy to man, without the support of his parents or a wider social network. However, he had his brother, other boys and he had his books. He also had plenty of determination.

It's also possible that the move to Ireland influenced Reginald politically. At the time, Protestant powers were weakening in Ireland with Fenian unrest. Eventually, the political unrest in Ireland was to affect the popularity of the school too, with the landowning and commercial classes that sent their children there declining in number. This was a time of economic slump in England and Ireland, agricultural prices dropped while the Irish crops failed, leading to the mass evictions of the Irish farming tenants who could no longer pay their rent. The Irish were outraged and as violence targeted at landlords rose, revolutionary parties such as the Land League and the Home Rule Party sprang up. In May 1882, Chief Secretary Lord Frederick Cavendish was assassinated on his first day of office. The response by Viceroy Earl Spencer was harsh, although it seemed to stablise the situation. Parnell, the leader of the Home Rule Party and the Land League, was jailed. On the face of things, violent repression had worked to preserve British rule in Ireland. Doubtless the boarders inside Middleton College were aware of the turmoil beyond the school gates and may well have lived in terror of the civilian unrest boiling over into their lives.

Aged 18, Reginald left Middleton and followed his older brother to the Royal College of Surgeons in Dublin. Around them, the Irish political scene was still problematic. The 'Irish Question', as it became known, beat two British governments and agitation carried on in the countryside, the ramifications of which continued to be felt even into this century. However, after a few months, Reginald gave up the idea of medical school and instead moved to the mainland to cram for the Army Entrance Exam for the Royal Military College (RMC) at Sandhurst. He passed – and so Reginald Dyer embarked upon a military career that would go down in history, though not for the reasons he had envisioned.

Sandhurst was highly competitive and had a punishing routine for its men. The day started at 6.30 and included parades, study, drills, riding, gymnastics and sword classes. It was a grand location – with extensive grounds and comfortable lodgings. Reginald's peers would have generally been of a higher social class than him, typically the sons of army officers, the aristocracy and the professions. It had a rigid code of behavior and trained its men to be an elite force that believed they were superior to the troops they would go on to command – and separate from the civilians they would meet. This attitude echoed the prejudice that he'd been brought up around in India and was to show itself time and time again in his adult life as he struggled to comprehend how anyone might dare to disagree with him.

Reginald passed out of Sandhurst in 1885 and was commissioned into the 2nd Battalion of the Queen's Regiment, which at the time was stationed in Fort William in Calcutta. It was a prestigious corps and a good start to his career. First however, Dyer was posted to Cork with the 1st Battalion of Queen's – just twelve miles from his old school. It was a steep learning curve for the new officer, as there had been rioting in Belfast in response to Gladstone's first Home Rule Bill. It was in fact the worst outbreak of violence in Ireland in the nineteenth century and lasted until September. Dyer and his battalion patrolled the streets in an attempt to protect those demanding home rule and suppress the Protestant factions seeking to maintain links to Britain and the Empire. It was a hard job, both physically and mentally, but peace was eventually restored and Dyer was then posted to the 2nd Battalion of the Queen's Regiment, with orders to deploy to Burma, arriving in Rangoon in late October 1886.

At the time the British army were fighting the 3rd Burma War, which was an attempt by Viceroy Lord Dufferin to land grab the remaining third of the Burmese state for the Empire. The land bordered British India and, with French interest suspected, the British wanted it under their rule instead. But King Thibaw – who still ruled upper Burma and Mandalay – refused the British ultimatum to hand over his territory and a bloody battle ensued, the king was exiled and the troops were merciless in their operations. A strong resistance developed, and more troops were deployed but the dense jungle battleground proved difficult to subdue. It took strategic planning by the experienced Commander-in-Chief of India, Sir Frederick Roberts, and an increase to over 34,000 men to finally grind down the resistance and remove the leaders. The troops were instructed to aim for the heaviest losses possible with the harsh policies eventually ensuring the pool of those prepared to fight the British invaders dried up, although it took several years to achieve this. Military might won the day – a lesson Dyer no doubt learnt and applied unsuccessfully later.

Civilians that had not offered any resistance were treated with more respect though and their religion and customs were allowed to continue uninterrupted. Leaders that were compliant were honoured and given local authority as recompense and troops were banned from touching Burmese property. There was an amnesty and rewards for those that surrendered. During his time in Burma, Dyer was given a detachment of men to command in an isolated post. With no close supervision, he was able to make his own decisions about how the army behaved and how the natives were treated. It's likely anyone would enjoy the freedom this afforded, let alone a young man desperate to prove himself.

Dyer left Burma for India, complete with a campaign medal and two clasps – and a reputation for bravery and dash. This would have been a great start to his military career had he not become involved in a scuffle on the steamer out of Burma. A disagreement arose between his bearer and the vessel's crew. It escalated to the point that the captain of the boat filed a complaint about Dyer once ashore. While Army HQ did not make a note of the issue on his record, it's clear it was an example of Dyer losing his temper when faced with native disobedience. It had not occurred to him to back down at any point.

After arriving in India, Dyer returned to Simla and saw his childhood home and family for the first time in twelve years. His parents were living a quieter life since his other siblings had left home but the brewing industry had prospered and the Dyers senior now spent the winter months in Lucknow in an old rajah's palace. During this period, Dyer sat and passed the Urdu exam that was required by the Indian Army and was successful in his application to join it. He received a probationary commission as a Lieutenant in the Bengal Staff Corps, an infantry role. His first posting was to Cawnpore with the 39th Bengal Infantry at the end of 1887.

It was not an illustrious start as morale was low in the regiment, with the mainly Hindustani men being phased out in favour of other races which were considered more warlike. The regiment was placed under review when a soldier used the regiment Standard to retrieve his shoe from some mud. Cawnpore was infamous for its past too – British women and children had been massacred there during rebellion and the bloodstained hooks where children had been hung remained, along with a well where bodies were thrown. Cawnpore was an open wound for the British, one Dyer seemed particularly affected by. It also seems that choosing the infantry above the cavalry upset Dyer's mother, and their relationship began to deteriorate, although what kind of relationship one has with a parent you last saw twelve years earlier as a child is questionable.

The 39th were posted to Jhansi, a long, slow but pleasant journey of one hundred miles. Colonel Ommanney travelled with the troops and brought along his wife and their two daughters. The older daughter was called Anne Trevor, known as Annie. Romance blossomed between Annie and Dyer; they were engaged by 1888 and went on to have a forty-year marriage until Dyer's death. With a distinguished record of army service both in England and India on the bride's side, Dyer was definitely marrying up, but for some reason his mother was against the wedding and his relationship with his parents was irrevocably damaged over the issue. It was agreed that Dyer would receive 100 rupees a month for his first year of marriage but then would not see any more financial support from his parents; he would need to make his own way financially. Dyer and Annie were married in April 1888 and spent a short honeymoon in Lucknow. His parents did not attend and he never saw them again. Perhaps this turn of events was a reflection on how independent he had become from his time away at school and Sandhurst – and also an indication of how he was able to cut off emotionally from people if they did not agree with him. Surely no one can walk away from such a damaged relationship with his or her parents without some emotional impact?

After their honeymoon Dyer joined the 29th Punjab Infantry at Peshawar, and Annie joined him, which she continued to do throughout his postings whenever she could. Peshawar was an exciting trading town and there were constant operations to ensure the border remained secure. The regiment was well regarded, and it was here that Dyer met many Sikhs and learnt about their religion and their language. After five months, Dyer was dispatched to the tribal lands of the North West Frontier, which was prone to sporadic outbreaks of violence. His campaign was a successful one – centred in an area called the Black Mountains – and it brought peace to the area for three years. It also earned Dyer a third clasp for the India General Service Medal he won in Burma and a note on his all-important army record.

After three years, in each of which he'd seen an active campaign, Dyer now entered a period without much excitement or opportunities to impress senior officers. He passed his probation, which allowed him to stay with the 29th, and was given responsibility for regimental training. It was during this period he was to have a further altercation with a native, who brought an action against him in a magistrates' court. The case was dismissed but perhaps shows how difficult he found it to tolerate disagreements with those he thought less of – be they natives, civilians or both. During this time, Annie gave birth to their first child, but sadly the baby died. Their second child was not to come until six years later.

In 1890, Dyer's regiment moved to Jhelum in the north of the Punjab, a quieter and smaller garrison. While there, he took the year's leave that he was entitled to, returning with Annie to England. He spent the time at the School of Military Engineering, from which he earned a distinction and also took a voluntary topography course, also gaining a distinction. It seems Dyer could not stop working on improving himself and was able to focus on his studies extremely well.

When he returned to India, the army had undergone a shakeup and Dyer now found himself part of the Indian Staff Corps with a new role of Quartermaster, making him responsible for his battalion's equipment, uniform, ammunition, stores, catering and rations. During this time, Dyer continued to work on his qualifications, passing the Officers Extra Certificate in Musketry, a further example of his continued desire for career advancement. His approach seemed to be working as he was asked to officiate as Adjutant, a job that carried prestige and power and that was usually reserved for the best officer of each generation. Unfortunately, at this point, Dyer's career progression began to stagnate as instead of continuing on to become the Station Staff Officer, as would be expected, he remained with the 29th for another ten years without promotion and was then on the receiving end of a series of unattractive posts. We can only assume this must have been very frustrating for someone who had worked so hard to progress and that the desire to be noticed and recognized as an exemplary officer may later have led him to make the most rash of decisions.

In 1893, the 29th battalion moved to Meerut in Bengal, a quiet part of the United Provinces, infamous to the British for being the birthplace of the 1857 Mutiny. Dyer took and passed another exam, this time the Captains' exam, followed the next year by a period of study for the Staff College Exam, undertaken during a trip to England. He also spent this leave learning French in Paris and became a father again. While this was undoubtedly time well spent, both personally and professionally, it did mean that Dyer was to miss out on the siege and relief of Chitral, which may have offered a chance to catch the eye of superior officers, garnering medals and perhaps a promotion. By the time Dyer returned it was too late to participate in active duty and he was instead absorbed into troops protecting the Malakand pass. He then returned to the battalion station to sit – and pass – the College Staff Exam, then accepting a place on the two-year course at Camberley, where he was to go in 1896, allowing him to be reunited with his wife and their infant son. During this time a second son would also be born.

In 1899, Dyer sailed back to Delhi in India, where the 29th were now based, to become Wing Officer of mainly Sikh soldiers. The battalion was posted to Peshawar, passing by Amritsar en route, where the troops had a stopover. It was during that time that Dyer became involved in yet another dispute with civilians when some of his men accused a local of peeping at their women inside tents and took matters into their own hands. Dyer settled the dispute and said he would investigate, but the soldiers were never punished, a sign that he regarded disputes with civilians as of no great importance.

In the years that followed, Dyer's career continued on and included some time posted in the regimental depot, which allowed him plenty of freedom to train recruits and supervise both Indian officers and seconded NCOs as he wished. He also spent a period, following army reforms, in charge of a double company. By 1901, he was sent to the foothills of the Himalayas to command a school for military officers in Chakrata. Here again, he was in charge of his own unit, far away from superior officers, allowing him plenty of freedom to work as he saw fit but with little chance to impress the commander and angle for a promotion. This five-year posting did allow him to settle into the role however, with his family beside him. It seems he remained a popular major among his students and would have received a rank promotion and pay rise in this position.

In 1902, the same year as his father's death, the military school moved to Meerut as the cooler weather set in. Dyer was called to act as a temporary staff officer in the headquarters of the 4th Brigade, which was on manoeuvres. By the summer of the following year however, he was back with his school and moved back to Chakrata. Now that his sons were older, it was decided that they should go off to school in England and that their mother would go with them. By 1904, Dyer was left alone and turned his attention to more studying, this time for the Q exam which he would have to pass (and did) to become Lieutenant Colonel. This was a time of political power play in the army, with Viceroy Lord Curzon and General Lord Kitchener, the Commander in Chief, disagreeing on the way the services were managed. Kitchener's reforms included the centralising of manpower – with the view to freeing up more personnel for operations and reducing overheads. For Dyer it meant his regiment, the 29th, became split up along the frontier, with his links to the battalion becoming ever weaker. This would have been a frustration for him career-wise, despite the fact he seemed well-suited to and successful in his teaching role. But he remained out-of-sight and out-of-mind when it came to prestigious promotions.

By 1905, his time in charge at Chakrata was over, and he took a year's leave back in England with Annie and their children, for once without taking on any extra studying. By 1906, he was back in Meerut as double company commander of the 29th at Jullundur in the Punjab, where it was necessary to work on the shooting skills of the battalion. Dyer now received news from England that his son Ivan had complications from pneumonia and was not expected to live. He took emergency leave to return home, where fortunately Ivan recovered. But perhaps the action was not without sacrifice as it has been suggested that to return home, Dyer had to turn down the opportunity to command the 19th Punjabis. Instead, when he returned, Dyer took up a new job as second in command at the school of musketry at Chungla Gully as Deputy Assistant Adjutant General. This was the school he had trained in, gaining a first class pass. Although it was a larger school than his previous posting, it was again out of the way, and not a place to get noticed. For Dyer's biographers, who are of course examining Dyer's life in hindsight and perhaps looking for his reasoning on 13 April 1919, this was just another in the series of career frustrations for him, in another location that carried little prestige and chance for honour.

At this point in his career, Dyer turned his hand to working on the design of the Mekrometer Artillery range finder that was proving impractical in the field and unreliable when needed. He spent the next eight years working through various designs for a better infantry range finder, using his own spare time and money, perhaps in an attempt to gain military recognition, although also perhaps because it was a challenging problem for the army that he felt he could solve.

While Dyer's life at this point was relatively quiet, the extended period of European imperialism in Asia was about to be disrupted. The Japanese defeated the Russian Empire and Indian nationalism was also on the rise. The reforms brought in by Lord Curzon – including the re-arrangement of the Bengal university system and partition there – saw political agitation, protests, political meetings and press criticism of the government. Bengali revolutionaries were behind terror attacks, murders and vandalism. To some extent, the events at Amritsar were the result of poorly thought out decisions such as these, made by people at the very top of Indian administration, who were perhaps more out of touch with the people than those at ground level. While it was Dyer's decision to give the command to fire in 1919, the tensions of the time were a result of frustration at this lack of political autonomy.

The political unrest grew ever closer to Dyer, and violence broke out in Lyallpur, a richly-irrigated agricultural area in central Punjab. The riots were a response to various reforms brought in under the Colony Bill introduced by Lieutenant Governor Sir Denzil Ibbetson. For the landholders, the changes felt like an attack on their rights. Trouble broke out in several areas and was only quelled when the authorities deported the leaders to Burma and stamped out press support. It's likely that Dyer was able to draw a parallel with the civil unrest he now saw in India to that he had witnessed in his schooldays in Ireland.

In 1908, a new chapter in Dyer's military career started. Having spent 19 years with the 29th regiment, it seems there was no option for him to become the commanding officer there, and he was instead moved to take charge of the 25th Punjabis. It was a serviceable regiment that had been created to fight the Mutiny of 1857. The regiment contained a number of Khattaks, a Pashtun tribe, and in typical form, Dyer set about learning their language. The regiment was stationed at Rawalpindi, and Annie came from England to join her husband in his new posting in early 1908.

But Dyer didn't have to wait long until he saw action with the 25th, as within days of arriving, the battalion was sent to fight tribal forces near the Khyber Pass. The Zakkha Khel had terrorized the frontier since 1905, with killings, kidnaps and theft their favourite activities. Their lands were close to Afghanistan and now they wanted political independence, presenting a manifesto to Ross-Keppel, the political agent in Khyber. By 1908, their confidence was increasing, resulting in an attempted kidnap of the British Assistant Commissioner. They failed but it did not deter them, and they went on to rob a Hindu merchant's house. Those in the area were incensed at the lack of control the British seemed to have over these marauding bandits and demonstrated outside the Chief Commissioner's bungalow. Lord Morley – the Secretary of State for India – agreed to send an expedition of over 3,300 men into the area. The 25th were in charge of guarding the lines of communication at the rear. The expedition was a success; with the tribe taken by surprise and overcome, a surrender soon followed. It was another example of how military might could quickly put down rebellion. And for his part in it, Dyer received the India General Service Medal in 1908 with a clasp marked 'North West Frontier 1908'.

In the next few years, Dyer was responsible for the arrangements for the regiment's 50th birthday, continued with his work on the range finder and took periods of leave in England and locally in India. The Commandant of the 25th supported Dyer's promotion and by 1910, Dyer was put in charge of the battalion. This was a high point in his career, and at the age of forty-five he became a Lieutenant Colonel. The 25th flourished under Dyer and he worked hard, as ever, to improve the company's shooting skills and sporting prowess. Around him India was changing, with provincial councils now open to Indians and the new Viceroy Hardinge also keen on reforms, like his predecessor Lord Minto.

Then came George V's accession and for the first time in the British Raj's history, a British sovereign came to visit 'the jewel in the crown'. The 1911 Imperial Durbar started with speeches of a new beginning in India; changes were afoot with the capital moved to Delhi; the partition of Bengal reversed; and natives more involved in the general administration of the country. Dyer's battalion provided the guard of honour at the Royal Garden Party at this time and he was presented to the King and Queen Mary, also receiving a durbar medal.

Dyer's next move was to Hong Kong when the battalion was posted there in 1912. The revolution in China meant the possibility of border threats and refugees, and the British Governor of Hong

Kong feared fighting could follow. It was a physically unpleasant first three months, camped on the dusty reclaimed land earmarked for the new railway. Hong Kong battled with malaria-carrying mosquitos and infectious diseases such as smallpox and bubonic plague. Life improved slightly when the battalion moved to the corrugated metal huts in Lai Chi Kok that would be their home for the next two years. The New Territories were still wild and undeveloped and the natives were not always pleased with their new British rulers, so the 25th manned a series of military posts along the border. After five quiet months, Dyer and Annie took leave and headed to Japan. The timing proved less than ideal as the Japanese Emperor died and the country went into mourning. Back in Hong Kong, trouble broke out with pirates attacking Lantau Island and firing at the new governor and his wife and later targeting the police station in Cheung Chau, another island. Dyer had missed out on active service again and then Annie became ill and had to return to England to convalesce. Further personal defeat for Dyer came when he had the opportunity to show his range finder to the army. Unfortunately, he did not get a working model ready in time, and the collection of lenses and prisms that he did have to show failed to impress. The army went on to choose a design based on simpler principles; his years of hard work had been wasted. He hadn't become the inventor he had set out to be and had yet to make his mark either in that field or in battle.

Dyer was still stationed in Hong Kong when war broke out in August 1914, and some of his battalion was earmarked as part of the general reserve for the territory. Dyer's second in command was appointed to command the reserve, while Dyer took charge of the rest of the men now based at the Happy Valley race course camp, later moving across the harbour to Kowloon. The 25th did not see any action during this period, a disappointment for any ambitious soldier and commander. Later that year, when his time to serve in the battalion came to an end, Dyer returned to Rawalpindi, probably regretting that his time in Hong Kong had not been notable.

By 1915, Dyer was back in India while Annie remained in England in a nursing home. Their older son was a subaltern in the Dorsets due to leave for the front in France and the younger brother about to turn eighteen and so able to enlist. Dyer's new role was Senior Staff Officer in divisional HQ, in the heart of the Punjab. This was again a good posting and suited Dyer's ability to deal with details, but it lacked the prestige or glamour that an officer might find if posted to France or Egypt at the time.

Unrest in the Punjab and in Bengal continued with several revolutionary groups operating, including the Ghadr group financed at the time by the Germans. Ghadr, and leader Har Dayal, had their origins in California, and sent thousands of Indians that had been working as labourers in the USA and Canada back to India to spread the group's message. It also tried to infiltrate the Indian Army to spread disaffection. British forces were well aware of the movement and often intercepted its missions, interning its leaders and rounding up supporters. Dyer would have been aware of the group when he arrived back in the Punjab and would likely have known that the group had also influenced some of his Sikh soldiers during their time in Hong Kong. Terrorist attacks in the Punjab increased to the extent that there were forty-five serious events by February 1915 in what was a previously peaceful province. One of the revolutionaries – Rash Behari Bose – set up his HQ in Amritsar and then Lahore. Those in administration could see that the subversive element in the area was organised and determined, and this may have given rise to the idea that harsh treatment was necessary if full control was to be regained. Dyer certainly subscribed to this view if his actions at the Jallianwala Bagh are anything to go by.

In each case of these outbursts of rebellion – both civil and from within the Army – the punishments were harsh. Soldiers and members of the public that rose up under the influence of Ghadr – and those that followed through with Fatwahs issued by the Turks once they joined the Germans – were often quickly executed or transported. Revolutionary leaders were also arrested, exiled or confined to their villages. Any radical press was closed down. The Defence of India Act, supported by the Lieutenant General of the Punjab, Sir Michael O'Dwyer, reflected this authoritarian approach to rebels. This is the culture that Dyer was operating within, as O'Dwyer was his ultimate superior. Notably, it was O'Dwyer who went on to vocally support Dyer after the Amritsar massacre, and was desperate to clear the officer's name. He may also have been able to clear his own name by association.

Dyer's career progression continued as expected and he was promoted to full colonel, passed out of regimental service and on to general staff. In February 1916, he finally got the great opportunity he had been waiting for when the Chief of General Staff at Army HQ, General Kirkpatrick, summoned him to Delhi and he was offered the command of the Seistan Field Force, operating in the area that was then East Persia. Here was a chance to showcase his leadership in active service, far away from any superior officers who might take charge of a situation he could prove himself in. This period of time was to be the pinnacle of his career and in 1921 he even wrote a book about his experiences entitled *Raiders of the Sarhad*. Some of his actions during this time however may also have foreshadowed what was to come just three years later, when he was once again given full freedom to make decisions alone.

At the time, East Persia was a neutral, independent country with both British and Russian influences. Sistan, an area within Persia that bordered Afghanistan, was British. Alongside threatening British oil interests, one of the ways Germany tried to hamper the British during the war was to cause problems within India – using Kabul as one of their bases – hoping to persuade the Amir of Afghanistan to join their side. The Amir was not impressed with the Germans and the enemy's plans were faltering by the time Dyer arrived. Dyer's orders were to round up any German agents still operating in Persia and prevent them from entering India to spread dissent. It was a straightforward mission but one Dyer would lose sight of as he looked for glory.

The Germans also tried to cause problems for British troops in Persia, focusing some of their energies on creating trouble among the Baluch tribes in South Persia. Since much of the area was vast, barren and parched, the tribespeople had long since developed a lifestyle dependent on raiding, the Damanis of Sarhad were particularly known for this. The supplies that were regularly sent to the British lines made for rich pickings and disruption to those supplies hindered the British in their mission to protect the East Persia Cordon. The tribes were in effect Persian (although it's likely they didn't regard themselves as such) and were therefore protected and governed by Persia. It seems that during his time in the area, Dyer chose to focus far more on these raiding tribes, rather than the German agitators he was sent to root out and eradicate.

Dyer made the difficult journey to his post at Robat as soon as he could and took over from the outgoing Commanding Officer who was in ill health, not an uncommon problem for British troops and civil servants working in India. He immediately began to redeploy the troops under his control and request more cars and machine guns, albeit piecemeal.

He also wanted to beef up his troops and decided that the locally-recruited levies would fit the bill. Unfortunately, his request to control the levies was denied. During this time, Dyer also began to try and avoid what he probably deemed as 'interference' from British ministers, embassy and consular staff and those working for the government of India, rather than the military forces. He set up his own intelligence operation rather than use the one already in existence and exploited the fact that communication channels were complex, travelling long distances, in his attempt to bypass any political orders. He also requested that the army make him a general so that he could have more authority, and he was accordingly promoted to local brigadier general.

Dyer began to make increasingly bold moves to achieve his aims, including signing a treaty with one of the tribes without any advice or support from administrative or political sources. He also received permission to attack the Sarhaddis and seize their capital. The ensuing six-month campaign relied heavily upon Dyer's arrogance and bluff, often convincing the opposition that his troops were far larger in number than they actually were. He threatened to destroy the cultivated fields belonging to the tribes to gain their surrender and seized the fort in Sarhadd. Dyer became determined to push deeper into Persia and bring the tribes under full control, despite there being no real need or an order in place to do so. As part of his plans, Dyer asked Army HQ if he could build Khwash as his base. His request was denied and the army instead sent Brigadier General Sykes to Bandar Abbas and Kirman, both near the Afghan border.

Tensions between Dyer and those who worked with him, began to spiral out of control. The British Minister in Tehran complained that Dyer did not keep in touch with the Consul and Dyer became dissatisfied with his second in command, Colonel Wilkeley. The government also refused to pay a member of the Narui tribe Dyer had recruited as a spy, although the general still kept him on. Despite all this Dyer forged ahead with his plans, even holding a durbar at Kacha asking tribal chiefs to sign an agreement that saw them supposedly handing over land in return for money. No British political officers were present to officiate the agreement and there's no official record of the treaty. The agreement failed and within a few days, the tribes were raiding again, threatening to seize the Khwash fort that they now realised was only protected by a small garrison. Telling HQ that he needed to return to Khwash for health reasons, Dyer had to make a desperate journey back there in an attempt to reach the fort ahead of the attackers. He made it by the skin of his teeth and had to rely on stories about his car having magical powers being circulated by friendly Reki tribesmen to talk around those camped outside the fort, who were more than ready to attack.

Once again, the authorities tried to rein in Dyer. Shortly after this event, he was told that Major Hutchinson, the Political Agent for Chagai had been appointed for political advice and that he was to consult with this officer before taking action and, in the case of any disagreement between the two, he must report back. He was also told to keep the Agent to the Governor-General in Baluchistan and Brigadier Sykes in Bandar Abbas informed and to act on the advice provided by the Consul of Seistan and Kain. He was also reminded that he was not in charge of the Seistan and Hazara levies and that the Political Agent in Sarhadd was to control the Sarhadd levy force. His role of training levies and operations – and its temporary nature – and the fact he was there to capture Germans was reiterated in an attempt to control Dyer, force him to work within a team and to ensure he listened to the advice of non-military staff.

Reminders, however, seemed to have limited success. Dyer continued to switch troops to the South and to Khwash, to the extent that army HQ, the Russians and even the Secretary of State for India expressed concern that the deployment would weaken the all-important cordon. He turned his attention to the building of a road to improve the route for supplies and to finding a summer station for what he clearly considered his army, hiring a gardener for the fort and re-designing its building. He even asked for uniforms and better weapons for the levies (but was refused). He was clearly not listening to the repeated attempts to remind him of his initial mission and to listen to the civil and political staff skilled in negotiation and relations, which he clearly was not.

With his soldiers and service animals often on half rations, when one of the thwarted tribal chiefs deliberately burnt crops Dyer had arranged to buy for his troops, trouble was inevitable. Furious, Dyer ended up in a heated argument with the Baluch, taking thirty-nine of the tribe prisoners, including the Chief himself. Since this caused local ill-feeling, Dyer wanted to send his prisoners to Quetta, asking Division for an escort, which they agreed to send, along with three hundred soldiers who were working on the construction of the road between Rabat and

Nushki at the time. The escort would however take two weeks to arrive, so instead of sitting tight, Dyer decided to send the prisoners off early to meet the escort along the way, led by a Captain James. On the first night away however the majority of the prisoners escaped, leaving only the chief, his son and two others in captivity.

Reprisals for the original capture by the escapees and a rescue mission for the Chief left behind seemed inevitable, leaving Dyer in an unenviable position. Dyer now realised that not only were his men and the escort they were due to meet in danger, but that a separate convoy with a consignment of gold coins headed to Khwash from Ladis was also at risk. Dyer decided to take some of James' men and some from the fort and set off to the tribes' central territory. He told James to head towards the gold escort. However, Dyer misjudged the raiders' moves and they attacked Captain James, the remaining prisoners escaped and the British sustained heavy losses. Dyer returned to the fort, requesting reinforcements for an expected attack there. Together, Dyer and his reinforcements were able to retain the fort, but the episode put Dyer in the doghouse with Simla. Dyer had made a catalogue of mistakes that included not waiting for the escort, underestimating the value of the chief as a prisoner, heading off in the wrong direction and losing face for the British. He lost further respect when during an investigation into the events, he tried to blame Captain James and exonerate himself. His plans for glory were not going well.

Problems with the tribes – and the chiefs with whom he had clashed – continued into the summer of 1916, as Daminis began to surround the fort at Khwash. Reinforcements arrived for Dyer in the form of the detachment that had been escorting the gold, Captain James and the men left with him – and what remained of the prisoner escort party – along with the new Political Agent for Sarhadd, Major Hutchinson. Perhaps unbelievably, after just two days Dyer set off again to hunt down tribal leader Jihand Khan and the tribes that left the area once reinforcements had arrived. Another arduous journey started for Dyer and his men; this time he was suffering from dysentery and conjunctivitis. When the British forces stopped at Gusht Fort, the Baluch attacked from the high ground forcing a retreat and several days of fighting until Dyer got the upper hand and the tribes fled. Again, the soldiers and their animals were suffering from lack of water and exhaustion, but Dyer pushed on, eventually losing many camels, goats and sheep before reaching Khwash on 29 July.

After four days rest this time, Dyer planned to set off to hunt down the Gamshadzay people. Major Hutchinson advised against it, preferring a diplomatic approach, but Dyer instead set out to an arranged meeting at Gusht with Major Keyes, who was responsible for the area to the South. Once there, Keyes arranged a durbar with the friendly tribes hoping to improve relations through restraint. Again, this was not enough for Dyer who wanted to punish the two sections of the Damani tribe that refused to recognize his authority. At Jalk, the Amir Madad Kham also tried to broker a deal between Dyer and friendly Baluch. But Dyer's terms were too demanding and no agreements were reached. Dyer was in danger of damaging the relationships the diplomats had cultivated. He planned a secret mission to attack Jalk, hoping to round up dissenters, but found them all gone, bar women and children, who he released.

It's fair to say that his original mission – to protect the cordon from infiltration by Germans – had long since been forgotten. To many, it began to look as if Dyer was hell bent on expanding British territory in Persia, particularly because, despite having been told to retain the base at Robat rather than Khwash, he continued extending the latter and even the road towards it. He also created hostility in many he worked alongside, not least because he so carelessly damaged delicate relationships others had worked hard to develop. The Afghan Amir and Persian Government also began to feel unsettled by his actions, fearing the annexation of Persia. Sickness and hunger spread across the areas Dyer had ravaged too; during his reckless and self-justified campaign, his army had killed many men and animals and devastated local agriculture, displacing families and destroying livelihoods, leaving hungry refugees at risk of disease in his wake.

But Dyer remained stubborn to the end, staying in Khwash as long as he could despite dwindling supplies for himself, his men and their animals. When HQ could no longer replace the vast amount of camels Dyer's supply caravans required but continued to push to exhaustion, a piecemeal withdrawal reluctantly began. The tribes never surrendered fully to Dyer, and instead he was forced to return to Simla because of his ill health, a move he expected to be temporary but that the army decided would be permanent. It's likely that his bout of colitis spared him the professional embarrassment of being removed from his post more directly. Conversely, he did receive a mention in dispatches and was made a Companion of the Order of Bath (CB) for his time in Sarhadd, which sent out a mixed message as it is also thought Dyer's careless actions in Persia adversely affected his future career prospects. If he knew this, it might go part way to explaining why he was so desperate to be the hero he thought he was in Amritsar a few years later.

After Sarhadd, Dyer was recalled to Simla and then temporarily posted as brigade commander in Abottabad, close to the Kashmir border. Within a few months of taking up the position, a horse he was riding fell on him and he was granted six months leave in England to recover. He returned to Annie in Suffolk and with his characteristic determination worked hard to recover full use of his legs, which had been badly damaged and affected his ability to walk properly. There's no doubt this would have been a long and frustrating process – and potentially a painful one too. Things may have been very different if he had given up at this point or decided to put his army career behind him, that is if he could have afforded to. Instead he was passed fit to return and shipped back to India for permanent command of the 45th Infantry Brigade at Jullundur in the Punjab.

But India was now a changed place, with plans for reform announced by Montagu and ideas of a decentralized government and more Indian representation being discussed. British India was still divided in its opinion though, and the political backdrop and the First World War meant that many of the plans for Indian self-rule were often watered down or delayed. Many British Indians were not happy with the changes, and this led to racial tension. While some clubs began to let Indians in, the Jullundur Club in particular refused to let in Indian Officers, who could now hold the same rank as their white peers. Proving that military status was of paramount importance to Dyer, and that he viewed those in the army superior to any civilians – regardless of skin colour – Dyer resigned from the Jullundur Club in protest.

At some point running his large brigade in Jullundur, Dyer learnt by letter that he was not suitable for further promotion in the army. Perhaps, as he went through the peacetime routine of drills, parades, paperwork and social events, Dyer wondered how he might find a loophole to allow career advancement, as he was not one to accept no for an answer! He may well have come up with the idea that he needed a bold move to prove his worth, one not often available when there was no active service and battles in which to demonstrate your abilities.

The Dyers' niece Alice joined him in January 1919, although it was an unsettled time to arrive. With the Montagu-Chelmsford reforms faltering and the Defence of India Act expiring, the security of India was under consideration. The controversial Rowlatt Commission was formed and decided that internal terrorism remained a threat, concluding that wartime special measures should be kept in place. This allowed the Viceroy certain powers, curtailing the usual legal processes and meaning provincial governments could potentially intern suspects. Interestingly, the Rowlatt Act of 1919 went on to be repealed three years later and its provisions were never needed or used. Unfortunately, the Commission and its conclusions may have unwittingly set off a chain of events that resulted in the shooting at Amritsar in April 1919, and ultimately in more loss of life than they could have imagined.

Amritsar was the major city in Dyer's area of command and was just a few hours away from Jullundur by train or road. Lots of political meetings were being held there at the time, covering everything from local issues such as station platform tickets and council elections to the Rowlatt Act. Dyer would have been aware of the meetings and the general feeling of the people. It is less clear whether he actually agreed with or cared about any of the controversy. In any case, since his military life was fairly settled at the time, he headed off on a ten-day road trip with Annie and Alice. The holiday happened to coincide with the *hartal*, or strike by closure of shops and work places, called by Gandhi on 30 March, where the trio witnessed some of the unrest attributed to the agitation, found many of the places they wished to see closed and also encountered some hairy moments, such as when their car was targeted.

While the *hartal* on the 30th had been peaceful in Amritsar, in advance of the second on 6 April, divisional HQ in Lahore briefed Dyer to guard the station, telegraph offices and the bridges and culverts of the railway, which was particularly important, as it was the line to the frontier. One poster pinned to the clock tower read 'prepare to die and kill others' but there is no evidence to suggest that any violence was pre-planned. The British administration remained worried however, as the trend for Indian classes and religions to work peacefully together against the Raj was unexpected and unfamiliar. The paranoia in which British India had lived since the Mutiny with was never far from the surface and in fact it seems that Dyer was not impervious to this himself. Fear that the crowd would rise up and overwhelm his men in the Bagh on April 13 may have played some part in Dyer's order to fire for a full ten minutes at those gathered in the Jallianwala Bagh; it was certainly his defence for the shooting at some point, although his account was changed over time and as it suited his audience.

After the shooting in Amritsar in which Dyer ordered his men to fire on unarmed civilians without warning and then left the dead and wounded where they lay to return to his HQ, Dyer found himself sent off to deal with problems that had now arisen in Afghanistan. At this point, Dyer and his supporters probably didn't realise how controversial the shooting at the Jallianwala Bagh would become. Much of the Punjab was quiet because it was under martial law, and it might have seemed as though Dyer's order to fire had successfully put down rebellion in the region for good. But there were certainly some people who thought his actions had been unnecessary and that his version of events left a little to be desired. However, it wasn't until much later that the Hunter Committee would call into question the details of 13 April, and even longer before the far-reaching effects of Amritsar would be analysed.

While the Punjab region was working through its post-war unrest, across the border, the Amir of Afghanistan, Habibullah, had begun to re-think his foreign policy. During the First World War, Afghanistan remained neutral out of loyalty to the British but now, Habibullah pressed for independence in his foreign affairs. The country had sheltered but not supported Indian revolutionaries during the war, and anti-British voices, including from within his family, grew louder. Following Habibullah's death while hunting, his son Amanullah usurped his uncle and announced his succession as Amir to the 'free and independent government of Afghanistan', an announcement the British did their best to ignore. But Amanullah was not satisfied with just words and decided he would use a battle with the British to win back popularity with his people, perhaps gaining back some the territory previously lost to the Empire to add to his résumé.

Expecting a disheartened India to rise up in support of the attack, Amanullah sent troops to the frontier and accused the British of murdering his father. In a breach of the treaty on foreign policy Afghanistan held with Britain, he sent envoys to Teheran and Bokhara, at the time a central Asian state in its own right. He also held a durbar on 1 May, reading aloud letters from aggrieved Indians under British rule and had anti-British leaflets distributed in British areas of the frontier, supporting murder and vandalism. Three days later, Afghan forces occupied Bagh on the British side of the frontier, killing labourers who were working there and effectively taking control of the water supply to the Raj's Londi Kotal station. In response, the Government of India ordered mobilization of troops on 5 May and cancelled the post-war demobilization that had begun. The British demanded that the Amir arrest the Afghan commander at Bagh but Amanullah refused, instead calling the Rowlatt Act a 'tyrannical law'. The Amir went on to call a grand assembly of all the Afghan troops and declared a holy war against the British. In return, Britain declared the third Afghan war on 6 May.

Amanullah first planned an uprising in British-controlled Peshawar, hoping to set his army to make three attacks, one each in the northern, central and southern areas of the frontier. The Afghan had hoped to capitalize on unrest in the Punjab, although he missed his window of opportunity as martial law had been so widely applied. A spy thwarted Amanullah's initial rebellion in Peshawar however by tipping off British intelligence to the plan, and instead the ringleaders in the town were rounded up, troops surrounded the area and the water and electricity supply was cut off. The British also pre-empted the southern attack despite the army not being at full strength and somewhat low in morale following the end of the First World War.

In fact, when Dyer arrived in Peshawar on 24 May leading 45 Brigade, it was to a fairly routine post, with the Afghan war seeming an easy win. Things changed rapidly though when the Afghan General Nadir Khan unexpectedly drove a force across from Mutan, an area generally considered impassable and therefore left relatively unguarded. This was an attack in the central frontier area, inhabited by volatile tribespeople who had no particular loyalty to the British. The tribes joined the Afghan army and the British were on the back foot, unable to defend their lines. The Afghans reached the British post of Thal, with British soldiers effectively under siege as the enemy almost surrounded them. In a stroke of fortune for Dyer, who lived for active service, he was instructed to take his men to Kohat to become part of the newly-formed Kohat Kurram Force.

The Thal Relief Column, as it became known, assembled at Hangu as there was only one route into the outpost. The troops and their supplies and equipment were ferried by the train to the end of the line there so that they could be in position as quickly as possible and in as rested a condition as they were able to be, given many were war weary. It would be a long, dusty and hot march to their destination as lorries were in short supply to carry the 2,612 men they had amassed to fight the invaders. On 31 May, Dyer set out for the first day's march, making it the longer of the two. It was eighteen miles in distance, with limited water and even Dyer, who marched alongside his troops, passed out through heat exhaustion. They reached Darsamand and camped for the night, facing only half as much walking to Thal itself the next day.

The enemy they faced was six times the size of the British troops but Dyer had the upper hand in strategy, support and intelligence, although his own health was faltering. Dyer decided to attack the three positions held by Nadir Khan in turn. He didn't have the manpower to attack all three simultaneously but luckily the positions were too far apart to help one another. He instructed Colonel Houston to attack the enemy on the south of the fort, which was made up of tribal allies rather than Afghan troops, an order he just managed to give before collapsing. The operation went well and the enemy was sent packing. Later in the afternoon, Dyer's force then attacked the Afghan guns hidden at various points. In a bid to not draw fire upon themselves, the gun points that survived this assault ceased firing. Dyer rested his troops overnight, which afforded many of the tribal forces an opportunity to abandon their posts. When Dyer put the final part of his plan into action the following day, the Afghans fled the scene. Nadir Khan sent a message requesting a ceasefire, but Dyer forwarded it on to Division while continuing to send more of the enemy soldiers on their way.

Dyer had wanted to push on further but was reined in by superiors and told to rest his men instead. The troops were exhausted and cholera had broken out following the unsanitary conditions of the siege. An Armistice was signed on 3 June and a ceasefire proposed. The war had lasted just twenty-nine days, with minimal losses on the British side. General Dyer's Relief of Thal had been a resounding success and much was made of thanking officers and troops. While the battle was won, the war for independence was effectively lost as, later that year on 8 August, Afghanistan was granted independence in its foreign policy. For the Afghans, this was a victory, and later, Nadir Khan was to seize control from Amandullah in a coup. The frontier remained somewhat volatile until 1924.

His work in Thal was to be the most successful campaign of Dyer's career. He faced an enemy that far outnumbered his own troops, rescuing a garrison under siege in challenging physical conditions. He took quick, decisive action that was well thought-out and strategic, inspiring the war-weary troops he had available in a textbook manoeuvre that only sacrificed a few British lives. This success must have been something Dyer held on to tightly in the next few years, as his actions at Amritsar were called into question.

Following an extended convalescence after Thal, Dyer only rejoined his brigade when it was stationed at Chaklala, as a reserve army for the Mahsud Campaign, which saw independent tribes attempt to assert themselves after the Afghan war. The conditions were spartan, but Alice, who was engaged to Dyer's staff officer Captain Tommy Briggs, went along to the tented encampment too. Dyer's health failed to recover however, and when the brigade headed off to Bannu in the Khyber, Dyer was instead posted back to Peshawar. It would not be long before Dyer found himself at the centre of the Hunter Committee's inquiry, out of a job and then on a hospital ship headed to England, which he would make his home.

Dyer was diagnosed with arteriosclerosis shortly after his return to England, and by 1921 he had suffered a stroke that left him partially paralyzed. While he recovered enough to leave hospital, his life was never the same as he remained an invalid, unable to walk and needing constant care. In 1925, Dyer and Annie moved out of their son's dairy farm to a secluded cottage in a quiet village outside of Bristol. Much has been said about his final few years and that although he maintained it was his duty to shoot at Amritsar he was tormented by what he had done. The lack of clarity over whether what he did was officially sanctioned also probably left him with some doubts, although he maintained he had crushed a rebellion with his actions. Dyer died on 11 July 1927, after a second stroke. The last words he is quoted as saying are, 'So many people who knew the condition of Amritsar say I did right...but so many others say I did wrong. I only want to die and know from my Maker whether I did right or wrong.' His family, caregivers, local dignitaries and former military comrades attended his funeral in London. His coffin was draped in the Union Jack from Dyer's HQ at Jamrud, carried by a gun carriage and flanked by soldiers. It was a grand spectacle – and a political statement, documented in papers across the globe.

The myth of Dyer as the 'Butcher of Amritsar' often casts him as a crazed individual, an innate racist and a brutal killer. But he also represents the callous characteristics of the British Raj. His legacy was a controversy that rages on and the setting in motion of a chain of events that would serve only to ruin the relationships that, ironically, held together the British Raj that he so loved.

Chapter 5

Before the Massacre

The Punjab – the 'Land of the Five Rivers' – was one of the Raj's most valuable regions within India. It had provided the most army recruits of all the Indian provinces, with 100,000 Punjabis already serving in the army when the First World War broke out and a further 110,000 men raised in 1916. It was therefore a crucial element of British military superiority. The area also afforded rich agricultural supplies. Accordingly, problems within the Punjab were likely to be taken far more seriously than those in other areas.

Amritsar was an important city within the Punjab and by 1919 it had a cosmopolitan mix of 160,000 citizens, including Sikh, Muslim, Hindu, Kashmiri Muslims and northern Indian Hindu merchants. Many were well educated and many opportunities in the city were tied to the successful textiles industry. Sitting on a key junction on the mainline railway to the North West Frontier, Amritsar is also home to the breathtakingly beautiful Golden Temple, the centre of the Sikh religion. The temple was and remains a pilgrimage site for Sikhs as it houses their holy manuscript the *Grant Sahib*, which is kept within a smaller temple on an island and read continuously. The temple and its pavements are made of white marble, surrounded by a lake. Sikhs have been gathering at the temple since the eighteenth century to give thanks for the harvest and to celebrate their principal festival *Baisakhi*, or New Year.

In 1919 Amritsar was really two cities – the old and the new, native and European – separated by the all-important railway track. The old city, with its civilian Indians, was made up of narrow streets crowded with stalls and high buildings designed to keep out the sun. It was home to municipal buildings such as schools, banks, the police station and post offices. The newer British cantonment lay outside the city walls, and in contrast, was spacious, with wide, tree-lined boulevards. There was also a small garrison on the British side, with more troops stationed further away.

Amritsar was no stranger to controversy however, as it had been the HQ for revolutionary Rash Behari Bose, who successfully organised and masterminded terrorist attacks in Delhi and was behind the Delhi-Lahore Conspiracy of 1912, an attempt to assassinate the then Viceroy of India, Lord Hardinge, as the capital of British India was passed from Calcutta to New Delhi. Bose was also involved with the Ghadr revolutionaries and as a result, Amritsar was sympathetic to rebellion. The city had remained a political centre; a meeting of the All India Congress (the central decision-making assembly of the Indian National Congress) was due to be held there in December 1919, and the locals were known to support Gandhi's civil disobedience movement.

After the war, the Punjab, along with much of India, suffered greatly and Amritsar was no exception. Within the region, many men had fought for the British, only to see taxes rise sharply to cover war expenditure. In April 1917, a Super Tax was charged, a year later a new income tax, and by April 1919, residents were expected to pay an Excess Profits Duty. In Lahore, tax had increased by thirty per cent – but in Amritsar tax had risen by a staggering fifty-five per cent. While the cost of living had also increased dramatically – with food grains suffering a ninety-three per cent price hike for example – wages remained stagnant and many people were without work. Across India, bad weather brought poor harvests and looting and food theft rose. In the autumn of 1918, an outbreak of flu killed five million Indians (the 'Spanish Lady' pandemic went on to kill three to five per cent of the world's population between 1918 and 1920), swiftly followed by torrential rains and a malaria epidemic. In Amritsar, the war had brought the price of cloth down causing wages to drop, and many rural populations found themselves heavily in debt. These problems of hunger, disease and lack of security cut across all sections of society. This must have seemed a pretty poor thank you for the sacrifices the Punjab and India had made during the war.

The Lieutenant General of the area was Sir Michael O'Dwyer, who had little time for the natives – particularly those well-educated Indians who wanted equality. Using the Defence of India Act, O'Dwyer had censored and closed the local press and prevented local politicians from speaking out. But the Punjab was far from happy to remain quiet once the Rowlatt Act was passed. The press continued to report unrest and campaigns and the Punjab Indian National Congress was also very vocal, planning to hold a major meeting in Amritsar in November.

When Gandhi announced that the 30 March 1919 would be the first day of a politically-motivated strike, known as the *hartal*, the Punjab was happy to take up the call, closing offices, shops and businesses in peaceful protest. Amritsar also observed the *hartal* on the 30th without any violence – and mass meetings there attracted crowds that were over 25,000 strong. This included a large, open-air meeting in Jallianwala Bagh on 2 April, where Swami Daya Deo spoke about the concept of *satyagraha* and non-violence. It's hard to believe just under a fortnight later the very same area was the backdrop to such a violent act.

Indeed, many of the factors that led to Dyer's actions on 13 April 1919 were completely coincidental. And it is entirely possible that if certain things had been different, the end result might also have been so. For example, at the time of the massacre, Amritsar was in the hands of relatively new civilian leadership in the form of District Magistrate Miles Irving, who only took up his post in February of that year. In hindsight, many have suggested that he was ill equipped to deal with the political climate in the city at the time. His request for military help in early April certainly shows that he was worried by the support Kitchlew and Satya Pal seemed to elicit from the public, despite the fact that previous *hartals* had passed off peacefully. It was also unfortunate that Sir Michael O'Dwyer was not at all a shrinking violet and was happy to ride roughshod over anyone's ideas that clashed with his. Communication between civil and military leaders – and their inability to work together – also added to the tension that was an integral part of the chain of events. O'Dwyer's decision to deport leading agitators from the Punjab, was a major factor in what happened at Amritsar as it led to unrest and violence in the city, which in turn led to military intervention and the catastrophic conclusion, which we know as the Amritsar Massacre.

On 29 March, in an attempt to clamp down on local agitators, the Punjab government banned Dr Satya Pal from public speaking. Satya Pal had graduated from Lahore medical college and was from Wazirabad in the Punjab. He objected to the Rowlatt Act and became a leader in the fight against it. He was also somewhat of a symbol of Hindu-Muslim unity, as he worked alongside Dr Kitchlew to achieve their shared aims. Satya Pal had served in the army and was a keen follower of Gandhi, advocating non-violent protest. Unfortunately, clamping down on Satya Pal in this manner meant that his supporters became increasingly vocal in their criticism and this in turn led to resentment among the British.

This move had not only failed to prevent further unrest but also in fact increased the tension in the city.

Sadly, not recognizing that his actions were doing more to create than dissipate unrest, O'Dwyer continued his forceful campaign ahead of the next *hartal* planned for 6 April, banning still more leaders in Amritsar just two days before. These included Dr Kitchlew, Dina Nath, Swami Annubhava and Pandit Kotu Mal. Kitchlew was a Cambridge- and Münster-educated Muslim barrister, keen for political change. He was a khilafat activist (a political protest campaign launched by Indian Muslims to influence the British government not to abolish the Ottoman Caliphate), a local National Congress leader, a friend of Jawarhal Nehru and another supporter of Gandhi's non-violent approach.

Extra troops were also made available to Amritsar ahead of the 6th, to protect the precious railway hub should there be any trouble. Again, the *hartal* was peaceful but continued to shock the British administration as they saw Hindis and Muslims marching together and a Hindu politician welcomed into a mosque to speak. The British relied heavily on religious and caste divisions in society to reinforce their own position of superiority. The 'divide and conquer' strategy had enabled the British to drive a wedge between various sections of society and prevent them coming together in great numbers to confront the British as one.

Irving in the meantime tried to talk the other congress leaders out of observing the *hartal*, but Satya Pal and Kitchlew had secret meetings and proposed it go ahead in any case. The *hartal* was observed, and was peaceful, despite effectively closing the city, a move that worked to unsettle Irving further. In a showy response, the armed British garrison paraded through the streets, guarding the route to the European church. This in turn created more bad feeling, with *tonga* (a horse-drawn cart traditional in Amritsar) drivers refusing to carry British passengers. Feeling the pressure, Irving asked for reinforcements in case there was trouble, a request that was received too late to alter the events of the next few days.

British anxiety increased when the Hindu festival celebrating the birth of Ram on 9 April came around. The event saw Hindus and Muslims join together for the festivities in a peaceful but unusual 'fraternisation' that made those dependent on the divisive approach very nervous indeed. Muslims were heard shouting support for Gandhi and '*Hindu-Musalman ki jai* (Long live Hindu-Muslim unity)'. The city also began to fill up ahead of the *Baisakhi* horse and cattle fair on the 10th, as Sikhs celebrated the biggest event on their calendar, New Year. Despite no violence in evidence, rumours circulated that when Gandhi visited on the 16th, the natives would rise up to slaughter all Europeans. These suspicions and rumours combined with ongoing tension and lack of communication between various points of leadership worked like a 'How Not To' manual for peace and civil order. They also fed off the paranoia that had existed in the British Raj since the Mutiny.

In his characteristically decisive – but perhaps rash – manner, O'Dwyer decided to pre-empt any trouble, no doubt spurred on by the unease felt by his countrymen and women. In his defence, quick and aggressive action to put down rebels had worked for him in the Punjab region before but what he failed to recognise was that times had changed. He ordered the deportation of Kitchlew and Satya Pal, planning to have them taken from Amritsar to elsewhere in the Punjab. On the same day, 9 April, he ordered the arrest of Gandhi, who was due to visit the area. Gandhi was accordingly taken off the train at Palwal, on the borders, and directed back to Bombay. Kitchlew and Satya Pal were arrested the following day in a set up at Irving's bungalow, after having been invited there by the District Magistrate himself. The two men were taken by car to Dharamsalla in the hills, escorted by the police Superintendent, ironically leaving only the deputy in charge in the following days of unrest.

These actions were incredibly inflammatory – some might even say poorly judged. News of Kitchlew and Satya Pal's arrests reached the natives and 50,000 residents streamed from the city to British lines to demand the release of their leaders. By midday on the 10th, the crowd surged across the railway lines where British soldiers were stationed. When stones were thrown, the troops returned with bullets, causing casualties. The crowd became a mob, scattering and in anger finding any target they could. Railway buildings and property were wrecked and looted, a British railway man and garrison electrician were discovered and beaten to death. More railway and telegraph staff were attacked but rescued. The incensed crowd moved on and targeted the three British banks on the city's main street. Within the National Bank, Mr Stewart, the Manager, and Mr Scott, the Assistant Manager, were discovered, and in the Alliance, the manager Mr G.M. Thomson. These people were dragged out and burnt to death in a bonfire made from the buildings' furniture. Staff from the third bank, the Chartered Bank, were hidden by their Indian colleagues, and thus survived. During the rampage the banks, the town hall, the churches and missionary buildings plus the post offices were all destroyed. Attempts to cross the railway bridge were made but each time drew fire and the rioters failed. A total of ten Indians were killed, with thirty injured.

Any Europeans that the mob came across were in danger. This included elderly missionary, Miss Sherwood, who was trying to get the girls under her care safely back to their homes. She was violently assaulted in a street known as Kucha Kurrichhan and left for dead, surviving because some locals found and hid her until she could be smuggled to safety. The trouble continued on into the afternoon, with the city lost to violence, arson and vandalism. While the army still held the railways line from the rebels, women and children from the cantonment were taken with their servants to safety in the fort. Their stay there lasted a fortnight and was undoubtedly a terrible experience as it was cramped and unsanitary and they were all terrified of what had and what might happen. Guarded by Gurkha troops, it must have seemed that all their fears about marauding natives were justified.

As news of Amritsar's riots spread, rebels outside the city cut telegraph and telephone wires and pulled up railway tracks. Amritsar was gradually beginning to feel isolated. Since a show of superior force and strength was really the British Raj's go-to defence system, this must have been very alarming for those in charge. Just before communication was lost however, Captain Massey contacted Dyer saying that the government of Punjab needed military help and Irving declared he had lost control of the city. Hundreds of men and a medical team were gathered in response, and Dyer and Captain Briggs commandeered a train to take the British and Indian soldiers to the city. They wired back (via alterative routes) that reinforcements were coming – even though the next available train was not due until 1am – and left Major Clarke in charge of delivering the soldiers to Amritsar.

The angry rebellion continued to spread to other areas. More railways, their buildings and communication lines were damaged in the environs, including those train lines that led to Jullundur and Lahore. The troops travelling to Amritsar were delayed as torn up tracks had to be replaced as they made their way to the city, eventually arriving at 5.15am. As well as Dyer's reinforcements, originally ordered by General Beynon, other troops were arriving, sent by Major MacDonald and more on the say-so of O'Dwyer, with General Kitchin, the Lahore Commissioner, in command, accompanied by the Deputy Inspector General of the Punjab Police, Mr Donald and the Superintendent of Telegraphs, Mr Coode. This was fast becoming a cliché of 'too many cooks' as the lines of who was in charge became increasingly blurred between civil and military officials. It's certain however that Irving was happy to stand back while Kitchin asserted and assumed dominance. From the army, Major MacDonald was the superior officer, and took control, with Kitchin apparently handing over to him verbally at some point, thereby submitting – in practice if not officially – Amritsar to martial law from the 10th. Accordingly, MacDonald marched troops into the city to rescue Europeans trapped in the city, many of whom were inside the *Kotwali* (police station), where the police force, under guidance of just the deputy, had been conspicuous by their absence during the rioting. The soldiers also retrieved the dead bodies of the murdered bank staff. The streets were now quiet.

Despite Kitchin handing over to MacDonald, he was still in the background, advocating military measures and keen that any further gatherings be quelled with force. O'Dwyer supported this approach too, approving planes and armoured cars. Dyer's reinforcements arrived and were handed over to MacDonald, with Major Clarke returning to Jullundur to report back to Dyer that Amritsar was no longer in civil hands. The planes, an armoured train and two armoured cars arrived, as did more soldiers to man the fort. It seems machismo and bravery were all around – with the British better equipped than they had ever been. British soldiers were now on guard at every exit from the city, and after considering how to deal with future rioters, MacDonald asked for bombs and aircraft machine guns. Kitchin told Irving to issue a proclamation banning gatherings and warning that anyone disobeying the request would be fired upon.

Disseminating that proclamation was a harder task however. Irving handed it to a group of lawyers that had come to see him at his temporary HQ at the station. It is also thought that it was given to some students at Khalsa College, and it is believed that some professors went through the city to make the proclamation known. Without doubt, however, the British military had seen the proclamation and doubtless took it at face value, reading that they had the go-ahead to punish those that disobeyed it. There is some suggestion that MacDonald was not entirely happy with how the proclamation had been publicised, and that he might have been less keen than others to base military action upon it. Later of course, it would be proved that fools rush in. The lawyers who were given the proclamation were actually visiting Irving to ask for permission for the mourners of those that had died the previous day to bury their dead outside the city. Mourners were allowed to do so provided they used only two of the city's gates, no *lathis* (stick-like weapons) were carried and that the funerals were all over by 2pm. If not, they were warned, troops would be ready to open fire at 2.15pm. The Indian funerals passed off without any trouble.

During these Indian funerals, the British also buried their dead and evacuated some women and children to Rawalpindi. MacDonald marched troops into Amritsar city after the burials to reclaim the main street and the municipal buildings close by. The next day remained calm, and the military maintained control. Kitchin however took it upon himself to leave for Lahore, and upon reaching there complained to O'Dwyer that MacDonald was not aggressive enough, based on the respect he showed by waiting until after the funerals had taken place to enter the city. O'Dwyer seems to have agreed and instructed General Beynon to send a replacement in the form of the far more fiery-natured Lieutenant Colonel Morgan. It's likely Morgan was led to believe that Amritsar was still in rebellion and that MacDonald had failed to take charge. This misinformation was yet another poor decision that led to events spiraling out of control and in the end served to benefit no one.

At about the same time it seems Dyer was also heading down to Amritsar in the apparent belief that Divisional HQ had sent him to take charge. During the enquiry into the events, Dyer maintained his orders had come via telegram, although no evidence of that has ever been presented. It's true that communication at the time was difficult, both in a practical sense and because of the confusion between military and civil handovers. It's also possible that Dyer was keen to see action again and maybe saw a victory in Amritsar as a chance to make up for the blot on his copybook he had from his time in the Sarhadd. It would be quite an assumption however to suggest Dyer took it upon himself to take charge of the situation and make up receiving an order just to get himself in the thick of the action. The lack of paperwork to prove if Dyer was or wasn't sent there certainly suggests that some confusion existed and that after the massacre some people used that confusion to protect their own reputations, even if this was at the expense of those of others. However, it wouldn't have been the first time Dyer used a lack of clear orders and communication channels to do what he felt he needed to, hoping to explain his actions later. And it's also true that Amritsar was a key city in the area he commanded. He requested that the troops sent from Jullundur to Amritsar be replaced, in case of further trouble or there was a need for further reinforcements. Clearly, he did not think that the unrest was over.

Upon arrival, Dyer headed to the makeshift HQ at Amritsar station to meet Irving, Plomer, Major MacDonald and Captain Massey. Dyer claims this is where Irving handed over control to him and he assumed military control of over 1,000 troops from MacDonald. When Morgan arrived, Dyer pulled rank and placed the Lieutenant Colonel in charge of Indian troops, despite his having no authority to decide upon the role of an officer from another command. At midnight, Dyer entered the city, taking the Deputy Commissioner, Captain Massey and fifty soldiers with him. They returned with the Indian City Superintendent of Police, Ashraf Khan. Talks carried on until the early hours, arrests were planned and then at 2am the electricity supply to the city was cut off, despite the fact that the 11th had been a quiet day with no violence.

Back at the helm at 7am, Dyer moved the HQ from the station to the open space of the Ram Bagh outside the city. This park was shady and tree-lined and offered a lodge for Dyer to work from. He also created a striking force stationed here, reducing the men stationed at the railway. Tension was increasing, with rumours coming in about pockets of rebellion elsewhere. The return of Kitchin upped the ante, with more reports – true or false – of further violence and attacks. It's not unreasonable to suggest that this culture of talking up the situation went some way to influence Dyer's actions and that while Dyer ultimately gave the order to fire on the Jallianwala Bagh crowd, there were many who were guilty of encouraging his approach. Accordingly, when the army plane reported back that there were people gathering at the Sultanwind gate, Dyer decided to march troops there and deal with it immediately. He took over 400 soldiers with him, two armoured cars and Irving, Massey and MacDonald. While the crowd was belligerent, it dispersed when asked. Unfortunately, the gathering Dyer encountered the next day was not asked to leave, nor did it get the chance to.

After dispersing the crowd, the soldiers marched on to the *Kotwali*, stopping several times to announce that assembly of over five people was now illegal. With help from the police, the soldiers searched houses for suspects and found Bugga and Dina Nath, wanted for the violent murders of the 10th. Shopkeepers were asked to open back up but they refused, unless Kitchlew and Sataya Pal were allowed to return to Amritsar. Dyer, his troops and their prisoners returned to their new HQ. Once back, Dyer set to work on a proclamation, with the aim of making clear to the people that the army was now in charge of the city, and that new regulations applied. The proclamation explained that the military would now deal with any disorder, and that troops would be called to disperse any meetings and gatherings, as they were forbidden. Dyer clearly believed that Amritsar was now under martial law and that any rebellion would be dealt with by force. Unfortunately, it's not clear how well this proclamation was publicised as the atmosphere within the city meant that it was not practical to communicate it. Again, after the massacre, those involved disagreed as to how well known these instructions were to the general populace.

The rest of the 12th proved to be busy, with soldiers dispatched to neighbouring towns, and worries about army supplies setting in as traders refused to sell the British their wares. The city was quiet without any public gatherings and shops closed. However, behind closed doors at a local high school, leaders of the agitation did meet and decide that the *hartal* should be observed until their leaders were free to return to the city. Another meeting also went ahead, where Dr Kitchlew's aide announced a public meeting would take place the next day at 4pm at the Jallianwala Bagh. It was to be organised by Dr Mohammed Bashir and was under the Chairmanship of High Court lawyer Lala Kanhyalal (who later denied involvement). This was a political meeting, designed to discuss a series of resolutions and was not intended to be violent in nature. The resolutions were in response to the approach and behaviour of both local and national government, designed to show that the people were not happy with the Rowlatt Act and the deportation of local leaders. It was also expected to express sympathy for the families of Kitchlew and Sataya Pal and to distance itself from the violent rioting that had occurred. Once passed, the resolutions were to be sent to various local and national leaders, including the Viceroy and the Secretary of State for India.

The atmosphere in Amritsar and the Punjab was still unsettled. Violence and riots were seen in Lahore, Kasur and Jullundur, and more railway lines were damaged. Again, rumours circulated among the Indians – this time of mutinies, the loss of Lahore fort and the death of O'Dwyer. Feelings were running high but by the evening and during the night, things were quiet once again. It's unclear if Dyer knew at this point of the political meetings that had taken place during the day or that a large, public meeting was organised for the next day. The troops remained as quiet as the city itself, no more marches or patrols were sent and no attempts were made to regain ground while the populace slept. Detractors after the event suggested that this would have been a better time to regain control of Amritsar with far less bloodshed. However, regaining the city alone may not have been enough for the section of British India that felt that restless natives needed to be shown a longer-lasting lesson. Egged on by the likes of Irving, Kitchin and O'Dwyer, it's entirely possible that Dyer believed he was there to punish rebellion in a way that discouraged it from happening again and to prevent it spreading to other areas of the Punjab. It was not the norm for the military to come to the aid of the civil administration and in some ways, the situation was unfamiliar ground to both Dyer and the others involved in this situation. This lack of experience combined with confusion over his actual mission in Amritsar may have contributed to the inappropriate response the city saw less than twenty-four hours later.

Never one to let it lie, despite Amritsar now being calm, and several of the leaders arrested and deported, Kitchin returned to Lahore to discuss the situation with O'Dwyer. The result was that at 4pm on the 12th, it was announced that the Seditious Meetings Act of 1911 was to be applied to Amritsar. This law banned meetings being held if it were likely they would cause public disturbance. Whether the people of Amritsar would have been aware of this declaration is unclear. Dyer spent his evening – and the early hours of the next day – working on a second proclamation, which he apparently planned to issue at various points around the city the next day. It was given to Irving to translate into Urdu. In retrospect, Dyer might have benefitted from more sleep in advance of what was to come.

Chapter 6

The Massacre on 13 April 1919

During the night of the 12th and in the early hours of the 13th, rebels in Amritsar continued to cause disruption by damaging railway and communication lines around the city. This may have been a deliberate strategy to isolate those in charge of Amritsar from those who would have been able to provide reinforcements – and it may have worked to increase the tension felt by characters such as Irving and Dyer. An armoured train was sent to patrol and mend the railway and to disperse the rebels. Dyer was also forced to send some of his troops to guard the treasury at Tarn Taran about twenty kilometers away, which had come under attack. Some of the troops that had been sent to Amritsar were also recalled to Lahore, potentially increasing the strain on army administration.

Determined to have his proclamation heard and perhaps to reinforce the military presence, Dyer organised a march, with his soldiers in the column formation. An armoured car drove at the front with the city superintendent, his sub-inspector on horseback and the local tax official in a cart. Next was the town crier, who beat a drum each time the column stopped and waited for a crowd to gather. The soldiers came after on foot, and then by car Dyer and Irving, followed by another car carrying two British police officers. Dyer had left word back at his headquarters for more troops to be sent in if he did not return by 2pm, suggesting that he did have some level of anxiety about personal safety. The march lasted for over four hours, with Dyer and his men returning unharmed to Ram Bagh by 1pm.

This impressive procession wound its way through Amritsar old town, stopping at nineteen points along the way to wait for people to assemble to listen and then the town crier read out the proclamation Dyer had written the night before. It was read in English and Urdu, and then explained in Punjabi or Hindustani. A printed Urdu version of the proclamation was also given out. Although the march stopped at many key spots and road junctions, it did not take in the Golden Temple or Jallianwala Bagh areas, and again in hindsight, this seems rather foolish, as many people would have been in the environs at that time. If it was a deliberate decision, then it might have been to avoid confrontation, although Dyer certainly wasn't one to steer clear of trouble if he felt natives were challenging his authority. The proclamation was also later criticised for not making it explicit that the city was now under martial law, as it listed only civil servants (rather than military personnel) as the people to seek permission from if you wanted to leave the city.

The proclamation did make clear that the city was under a curfew of 8pm and that anyone found on the streets after that time would be shot. It also forbade processions in, around or outside the city and banned gatherings of more than four men, again stating they would be dispersed by force if necessary. Those that heard the proclamation would therefore have known that political meetings were not allowed and could be dealt with by force. While it's unclear how many people heard the proclamation and whether those people were merely transient visitors, and not those who later found themselves in the Jallianwala Bagh, it is likely that word was spread in the town to some extent.

However, reports at the time suggest that Dyer felt the crowd ridiculed the announcement and that some listeners shouted that the British didn't have the appetite to fire. There was certainly some heckling by the crowd, and this most likely angered Dyer. Perhaps worse still, behind Dyer's procession came two other men, also banging a drum and making an announcement of their own – that a 4pm meeting was to be held at Jallianwala Bagh. Again, police told the crowd that if they attended the proposed gathering they would be shot. The police also arrested several of the more rowdy members of the crowd and unsuccessfully tried to get shopkeepers to open their businesses back up despite the *hartal*. As he made his way back, Dyer was told about the meeting planned for that afternoon. It must have seemed to him that despite giving very clear orders to the inhabitants of the city, they were hell bent on disobeying him. A military man through and through, with an obvious superiority complex, Dyer must have found this insubordination by those he considered less than himself both infuriating and humiliating. Once back at his base, he began to consider his next move. It's clear that – contrary to what may have been said later in defence of Dyer's actions – he had plenty of time to plan his strategy to deal with the forbidden meeting.

Amritsar's Jallianwala Bagh was approximately seven acres of communal ground, empty and dry in April, but planted with crops later in the year. Almost a square, it was just over 180 metres long, and a little longer in width, and has been likened to the size of Trafalgar Square. Unlike the open public plaza in London however, the Jallianwala Bagh was surrounded on all sides by the blank, ten-foot high walls of local houses, making it completely enclosed bar five narrow entrances. The only features were a small shrine, a deep well and a few trees. Outside the Bagh were cramped lanes, usually full of stalls and people. Despite its lack of vegetation and shade, as it was a large open public space, it was customary for people to gather there as they rested after a visit to the Golden Temple, and since the annual *Baisakhi* horse and cattle fair, which attracted farmers, traders and merchants into the town had been closed at 2pm by police in case of trouble, more people than normal were congregating in Jallianwala Bagh that afternoon. These people, of mixed religions, were not there for political reasons or for rebellion. Many were unaware of local affairs, only a few were armed with the traditional *lathi* that was common to carry, and some were women and children. They were certainly not the aggressive agitators from the rioting a few days earlier. Some were even ignoring the speakers, playing card games, chatting and sleeping.

However, the political activists setting up wooden platforms for the expected speakers and poets were aware of the proclamation and of recent events in their city, in the wider Punjab region and nationally. The organisers expected crowds to gather as they had arranged for water carriers to work within them. The police in the Bagh at the time would also have known, although no attempt was made by civil or military authorities to close the area, move crowds out or to stop the meeting going ahead, despite members of the police force having been seen talking to those running the event. It is thought that around 20,000 people were in the square on the afternoon of 13 April although estimates vary greatly. Not one copy of the proclamation banning gatherings was visible there. Many have since argued that if those in charge had wanted the meeting not to go ahead, clearing or closing the area, announcing that the meeting was illegal and/or negotiating with the leaders to cancel or leave would have all been possibilities; options that may well have prevented bloodshed. Alternatively, the Jallianwala Bagh was also a ready-made trap in which to collect rebels and those Dyer wished to make an example of. Some people believe Dyer was well aware of this, although he did maintain he was unfamiliar with the Bagh and its enclosed design.

What is clear is that since Dyer had been told of the meeting as he returned from the morning's march, he had several hours to decide what to do next. He evidently expected casualties and perhaps anticipated the crowd might retaliate as he arranged for any Europeans within the city to be taken to safety beforehand. Police intelligence and a report back from a spotter plane reconnaissance confirmed the crowd and its size and that it was in the enclosed walls of the Bagh, something that Dyer must have noted. This means that the massacre cannot be explained away as a trigger-happy reaction to a dangerous situation Dyer suddenly found himself and his men in, and neither can it be justified as a response to a violent mob about to recreate the scenes that left Europeans and state property vulnerable to brutal beatings and violence. It is more likely that Dyer saw this gathering as an opportunity to take decisive action to end the rebellion of the previous weeks – and to show rebels that he meant business. On a personal level, he wanted to punish those who had mocked his proclamation and disrespected the British authorities. While he must have known the crowds were not the same people that had directly disobeyed him, it's possible that he viewed all Indian civilians as entirely interchangeable and ultimately expendable for his version of the greater good. In his eyes, the order not to assemble had been disobeyed and the people must face the consequences. In this frame of mind, at 4.15pm Dyer set off to Jallianwala Bagh.

In total, Dyer took ninety soldiers with him to the Bagh. This force was made up of fifty soldiers armed with rifles, half of whom were Gurkhas, the other half Indian soldiers from mostly border tribes, with forty more Gurkhas, armed with their traditional curved kukris, as an escort. He also stationed five troops of fifty men each around the area and outside the city walls, presumably as a backup option if things went wrong or potentially to pick off any escapees. He led the troops himself, either because he wanted the glory when the shooting was hailed as a success or because he did not want his orders questioned by those less single-minded. Irving did not come, although Morgan, Briggs and two British bodyguards accompanied Dyer in his car. Two policemen travelled in another car, and two armoured cars were also present.

When Dyer and his army reached the Bagh, it was necessary to leave the cars behind because of the narrow lanes and enter the area by foot through one of the alleyways. The soldiers filtered in to an area of rising ground and took aim. With the speakers only about fifty metres away, those at the back of the crowd were effectively at close range. Pandit Durgas Dass, the editor of *Waqt*, the Amritsar newspaper, was eighth to take the stage and had just started to speak, criticising the Punjab government for repressive actions, when the soldiers arrived at about 5.15pm. As people began to panic, one of the organisers, Hans Raj tried to calm them, announcing that the British would not shoot. He was wrong and, without a warning, Dyer gave the order to fire. Captain Crampton repeated it, and the troops opened fire.

Once the shooting began, there was immediate chaos and panic as the crowd tried to flee but found the exits few and far between. Many were killed by the crush, and bodies began to pile up. Still others tried to climb the walls, while some lay on the ground to avoid bullets, or played dead. Many tried to huddle together or flee, as the bolt action Lee-Enfield rifles were re-loaded. None of these actions were to prove successful as the riflemen simply aimed at both individuals and groups in an attempt to maximize casualties. Still more people jumped into the well in the Bagh, only to drown or suffocate in the throng. When groups of men gathered together and posed a possible (but unlikely) threat, they were also shot. The densest parts of the crowd were also deliberately targeted. The firing lasted for around ten minutes, with an estimated 1650 rounds of .303 Mark VI ammunition used. By the end, there was a mass of trampled and bloodied bodies, including children. Many wounded lay dying and unattended. And then, leaving just enough bullets to ensure their safe return to the Ram Bagh, Dyer summoned his troops and swiftly left.

Many more people had watched the slaughter from outside the Bagh, or from windows and balconies that opened out on to it. Some were even injured by bullets despite not being in the Jallianwala Bagh itself, suggesting that bullets either ricocheted from within the park or that observers were also targeted. People – often wives that knew their menfolk were inside the Bagh – ventured inside to help the wounded and search for their loved ones but with a darkening sky and a curfew imposed from 8pm, many victims were left there injured overnight, many probably to die in agony, with wild animals scavenging for flesh. More bodies lay strewn in the alleyways leading from the Bagh, as they had died from wounds sustained while escaping. Others that were injured made it to the limited and overwhelmed medical facilities within the city. Dyer and his men meanwhile were back in the Ram Bagh by 6pm, and that night the area was heavily guarded in case of violent reprisals. None came, and a shocked and grieving Amritsar adhered to the curfew, with the streets empty and silent.

Reports of Dyer's mood immediately after and in the few days following differ, but overwhelmingly show that his actions were planned and deliberate, designed to shock the population into submission. He may well have found the event disturbing and distasteful but clearly felt that military action was a necessary evil. He was never to change his opinion that what he did was required and that it worked to prevent further deaths of both sides by stopping continued rebellion. In a similarly harsh reflection on the importance to the British administration of the individuals killed and maimed during the event, the task of counting casualties was not even considered until over two months later. Later still, on 7 August, the Punjab government asked people to submit the names of those that had died so that they could record the figure. While the number slowly grew, many would not have reported a relative or friend for fear that they might too be branded a rebel and dealt with accordingly. It must have been almost impossible to trust an administration that had knowingly gunned down innocent individuals just to prove a point. Who knew what they were planning next in an attempt to enforce civil obedience? Relations hit an all time low.

In the November of 1919, as they began their investigation into the event, the Hunter Committee agreed upon a figure of 379 identified dead, 87 of whom were visitors from outside the city, with an estimated further 1,000 people wounded. The dead they recorded were made up of 337 men, 41 boys and one six-week-old baby. The total was disputed at the time – and is still disputed today. Gandhi, for example, was given one estimate that put the death toll at over 1,500 and if the crowd was close to 20,000 strong, it seems unlikely that only a few hundred would have been shot by professional armed soldiers in a crowded area from which they could not easily escape. Those that were wounded but recovered were also far less likely to come forward too – after all they had been identified as rebels on that day, what had changed? They probably felt lucky to be alive and/or continued to suffer from the trauma of what they had seen that day.

Irving, who had apparently slept through the massacre rather than attend it, sent news of the shooting to Lahore some time after 11pm that night. Clearly, no one was in a rush to report the events and it seems that the details were fed through in a haphazard – and irregular – way too. Gerard Wathen, the Principal at the local Khalsa College, insisted that Irving send more details and forced him to write a fuller report that he took to Lahore by motorbike himself. It was Wathen who then gave the information to O'Dwyer. The Lieutenant Governor in turn sent his own, slim version of events to the Government of India. The clean up operation was now to begin.

Chapter 7

After the Massacre

Sir Michael O'Dwyer, Lieutenant Governor of the Punjab, first heard news of the killings in Amritsar at 3am the next morning. He was woken by Gerard Wathen, and a visiting lecturer to the Khalsa College, Mr Jacob, who were concerned enough to ask O'Dwyer to travel to the city to see what had happened. Instead of visiting Amritsar however, the Lieutenant Governor, a known hard-liner, called Commissioner Kitchin and Chief Secretary J.P. Thompson to discuss the matter, and then dispatched Kitchin to Amritsar with a note for Irving complaining about Wathen. O'Dwyer also called General Beynon asking for an update; Beynon had indeed heard rumours about the shootings but had also not investigated further, only later sending a plane to report on the situation at dawn.

Dyer was not in a hurry after the massacre either; it took him six hours to send just a short official report of his day's work to his superiors. A cynic might suggest that this was to allow him to craft a piece that put him in the best light possible, without revealing anything that might become an issue under later investigation; a 'right to remain silent' situation, lest anything he said be used against him at a later date. A more sympathetic view might be that he was quite rightly shaken by what he had witnessed, despite it being an act he felt it was his duty to perform effectively. The short paragraph he sent became the basis for all the decisions taken by those in authority in the aftermath of the massacre and Dyer was not to provide any more details or alter his version of events for four months, when the government was repeatedly asked to confirm details.

Dyer's report detailed his proclamation procession; one can assume to demonstrate how he had made it clear that meetings were forbidden. He also stated he had heard that a meeting was planned but did not believe it would go ahead. His account then tells how he marched troops to Jallianwala Bagh but was forced to leave the armoured cars upon arrival because of the narrow alleyways, and so entered the square by foot. He then explains that he saw a large crowd, feared any hesitation would put his small force at risk of attack and so ordered his men to open fire and disperse the crowd. He added an estimate of two to three hundred casualties, says 1650 rounds of ammunition were used and that he returned to his headquarters at 6pm.

The report had many aspects notable for their absence, not least Dyer's intentions when he marched specially selected and prepared troops to the Bagh where he knew the meeting was taking place, and just how many people were gathered there due to police and spotter plane reports. It also omits any mention of the fact that he did not ask the crowd to disperse before firing, how long the firing continued for – far longer than was necessary to disperse the crowd, one might argue – and what happened to the casualties when the soldiers eventually held fire. It also introduces the idea that Dyer gave the order to fire because he feared that the crowd might attack his men. This was not entirely true, as he went to the Jallianwala Bagh with the intention of making good on the threat that the British would shoot those who disobeyed the ban on assemblies; the same threat that was openly mocked as he processed around the city earlier in the day. It is this point that Dyer later came to refute himself, denying that fear motivated the order to fire. His later accounts suggest he fired upon the crowd to 'give them a lesson' and to 'make a wide impression'.

Short as it was, O'Dwyer, General Beynon and the Punjab government accepted Dyer's version of events, and continued to do so, even as Dyer himself changed his story as time went on. With its minimal detail, it allowed minimal criticism, and General Beynon accepted it when it reached him at Division, responding that since now was all under control, Dyer should not take any drastic measures from that point on. Perhaps revealing that he did have some doubts however, Beynon also telephoned O'Dwyer to seek endorsement of Dyer's actions, which he received. That morning, still perhaps uneasy, Beynon double-checked O'Dwyer's approval by bringing up the matter at the Government House conference, and having it noted in the war diary. Beynon then sent a now infamous message to Dyer that read 'Your actions correct and Lieutenant Governor approves'.

Back in Amritsar, the city was mostly quiet, although vandalism to railway property and communication wires continued around the area.

Early on the 14th, many people visited the Ram Bagh to ask for permission to bury their dead and to ask if they could open their shops. Funerals were allowed to go ahead but were restricted to just eight mourners per corpse, and processions were banned. Commissioner Kitchin and the Deputy Inspector General of Police, Donald, visited Dyer to give their approval and to report that they believed a further revolutionary meeting would go ahead at the Golden Temple, planned by Sikhs. Perhaps they hoped to see more knee-jerk reactions from Dyer?

Thankfully, however, Dyer, with the help of Gerard Wathen, saw fit to deal calmly with this suspected insubordination. He sent for the temple manager, Sardar Arur Singh, who came with Sardur Sundar Singh Majithia. Dyer promised the men that the temple was safe and that troops would protect it from rioters. In turn, the Sikhs reassured Dyer that their community remained loyal to the British and no rebellion was being planned. This well-thought out response to information that was little more than rumour helped to prevent further military attacks on the city. It also marked a period when Dyer worked with the Sikh community, greatly favouring them above the local Hindu and Muslim groups, again a technique of divide and conquer that worked to prevent bloodshed at least in the short term. In fact, the official Sikh clergy of the Golden Temple later conferred upon Colonel Dyer the *Saropa* (a mark of distinguished service to the Sikh faith or humanity), sending shock waves through the Sikh community. By October 1920, students and staff of the Amritsar Khalsa College had called a meeting to demand the immediate withdrawal of the control of their places of worship from such leaders and formed a committee to bring about reform. More than eighty years later, the maternal grandson of the *Jathedar* (clergyman) that honoured Dyer sought an apology from the Sikh community, calling the presentation a 'panthic mistake', and thereby suggesting that the spiritual leaders of the time were misguided in their path (or *panth*).

The next task was for the administration to speak to representatives of the people in the city. Kitchin assembled 150 chiefs in the public library and asked them if they wanted war or peace, warning that Dyer was now in charge. He left so that Dyer, Irving, Rehill and Plomer could take centre stage, which Dyer promptly did, speaking angrily in Urdu to the attendees. He told his audience that the government was prepared for war if that was what the rebels wanted, but that if they wanted peace they must obey orders and open their shops. If they did not do as they were told, he added, they would be shot. Clearly the audience knew that Dyer was not making an empty threat this time; he also said that for safety the city would be patrolled and the water supply would be turned back on. Dyer headed back to Ram Bagh, fifty Gurkhas were put on patrol duty and a further proclamation was read out in the city, announcing the arrangements. The shops opened the next day and Kitchin left for Lahore, content that Amritsar was now under control.

After the massacre, Dyer and his supporters often cast him as the 'Saviour of the Punjab' or 'Hero of India'. They claimed that the massacre had stopped in its tracks the spread of rebellion through the region and the country, suggesting that the widespread cutting of telegraph wires for example showed an organised conspiracy, the ultimate goal of which was to unseat the British Raj. As well as his peers in British India and the Empire-proud British back at home, this view was supported by Irving, O'Dwyer and General Beynon who all subscribed to the view that Dyer's decisive action had given the rebels a short, sharp, shock and brought an end to unrest.

Under close examination, however, this was not the case at all, as the Hunter Committee later discovered. While Dyer's supporters painted a post-massacre picture of peace, the reality was very different – with the hours and days after 13 April bringing more and more civil unrest, including some violence. Inside the city walls of Amritsar of course, people were justifiably terrified – and grieving. It was forcibly repressed, the people too shocked and scared to stand against the authorities, something that today we would call a dictatorship. Further afield though – in its own district and across the Punjab region, more and more people joined in acts of angry retaliation. At Wagah, the station was burned, the telegraph wires cut and railway tracks were pulled up, derailing an armoured train heading for Amritsar. Jallo station was also set on fire and a day after the massacre two Manjha villages erupted in violence. Tar Taran saw a *hartal* and cut telegraph wires. Railway staff also went on strike after the shooting, with vandalism to the telegraph system in the Punjab increasing dramatically on the 14th and continuing until the 21st.

All the infrastructure of the Raj – effectively the symbols of the British ordered lifestyle – came under attack. In Rotak District twenty miles from Delhi, mobs targeted a train and damaged a bridge. On the 15th, troops had to fire on crowds attacking the station in Gujrat, as violence spread across the Gujranwala District. By the 16th, mobs in the area attacked other government buildings. *Hartals* and wire-cutting continued – some *hartals* were peaceful, showing that the massacre motivated those committed to non-violent protests as well as those who were simply too angry to do anything but physically attack the administration. Wires continued to be cut until 2 May as disorder swept across the Punjab. For weeks, Jullunder and Amritsar districts faced unrest and resentment, while martial law was even imposed in Lyallpur, eighty miles west of Lahore on the 24th. It seems that, before political spin was an identified concept, Dyer and his supporters were using it to re-frame the massacre as not just necessary but as a positive step towards pacifying political agitators, whether it was an accurate picture or not.

On 15 April, two days after Dyer ordered the shooting, the government of India officially declared that Amritsar was under martial law. O'Dwyer, who was actually due to leave his post in a matter of weeks, asked the Viceroy to backdate the law to 30 March – which was agreed – so that it would cover any 'offences' committed by the British in the run up to the massacre. A state of martial law gave the police greater powers of arrest and detention and allowed for harsher penalties to be dished out, requiring a smaller amount of evidence to be provided before a conviction. The Government also published a resolution about how it would restore law and order across the country, so was clearly worried that rebellion was still ongoing. Martial law was also invoked in several other areas where wires had been cut, a somewhat heavy-handed response to a fairly low-level act of resistance. Meanwhile, troops were still being moved around to protect equipment as it travelled, and to protect specific areas; another sign that there was a general lack of confidence in the 'peace' that the massacre had supposedly brought. The need to keep Amritsar under martial law – and make that official – plus the use of it elsewhere in the region begs the question; if the massacre had put an end to the violence, why was the army still in charge of law and order in Amritsar? And, in other affected areas, why was that role transferred to them after the 13th?

Soon after martial law became officially sanctioned in Amritsar, Dyer was appointed as its administrator, with much of the work delegated to Provost Marshal. Written to allow easy prosecution, the law also included sixteen new offences drawn up especially. These covered the use of arms against the state and the inciting of others to do the same. It also banned the assisting or hiding of rebels, the use of language that would cause rebellion, calling or attending a meeting of more than five people and made failure to report a seditious gathering and disobeying an order given by an officer acting under martial law offences too. Any act that threatened public safety or prevented officers doing their job was also outlawed.

Amritsar martial law was used to prosecute any illegal activities that occurred in the city after the 19th, as well as minor offences under normal law that took place there. Major cases, and those where the illegal activity had happened before the 19th were sent to the martial law commission in Lahore. Punishments in Amritsar could include up to two years in prison, a 1,000 rupee fine, both of these penalties or whipping. Martial law was only lifted on 9 June.

It was unfortunate that martial law was introduced at a time when the city was trying to return to some normality, with soldiers able to march in the city, even by themselves, without expecting trouble. It is also ironic that this approach to control the residents by fear and force would have been completely unnecessary if the massacre, as Dyer and the Punjab Government argued, had put down any insurgents. The regional government continued to request powers that allowed it to keep the area in subjugation, including requesting that the Seditious Meetings Act be extended to Jullundur and asking Dyer to send an armoured train to patrol the area. Amritsar was even quiet enough to allow the Gurkhas that had been sent there to be moved on to Peshawar. Water and electricity were also returned to the city.

While Dyer was officially in charge of the execution of martial law, the police carried out the day-to-day tasks of both investigating alleged offences – and providing the evidence. On 18 and 19 April there were eighty-six arrests, on the 21st, 150. By the 25th, orders had come to arrest all suspicious *sadhus*; holy men usually of the Hindu or Jain religions, and by the end of April, 350 arrests had been made. The police however were left unchecked and rumours were rife of extortion, sexual assault, brutality, cultural insensitivity and confessions extracted by torture. Suspects were typically held for up to seventy-nine days, with many then released without charge. While martial law may have been invoked to root out rebels and crush insurgency, poorly-implemented and left unchecked, it simply created a culture of fear, hate and resentment. Those in the city became less and less co-operative with the authorities, with those at the top turning a blind eye to the corruption and coercion.

Dyer was away from Amritsar much of the time. On 16 April, for example, he was called to Lahore to a conference held at Government House to discuss the handling of martial law. Organised by General Beynon, once there, O'Dwyer questioned Dyer further about 13 April. Dyer stuck to his original story; that he had given the order to fire as he feared his small force would be overwhelmed, but now added that he had since thought he might have been mistaken about the practicalities of that assumption. While his account did not explain the length of time shooting – and the reloading of guns during the massacre – O'Dwyer did not push for further explanation. Perhaps he was satisfied that Dyer had taken decisive action, whatever the reason and circumstance.

When he was in Amritsar however, Dyer did nothing to exonerate the British administration or rebuild relationships with the inhabitants of the city. His own behaviour was petty and unpleasant, showing disdain for the natives. He punished anyone that did not *salaam* – or bow – to him as he passed. He also ordered all the city lawyers to enroll as special constables, expecting them to pass on new instructions to the public and inform on anyone acting suspiciously, often giving them manual work regardless of age or health. This role prevented the lawyers from carrying out their own paid work too.

Perhaps the most spiteful action that Dyer took under the cover of martial law however was a punishment he thought of after visiting Miss Marcella Sherwood, still seriously ill at the Amritsar fort. Miss Sherwood had been violently attacked on the 10th, and left for dead in Kucha Kurnchhan, a street in the city. The day after seeing Miss Sherwood, Dyer announced at church (and later back at the fort) a special provision for the street – or as he referred to it – the 'sacred spot' – where the assault had occurred. It was to be guarded from 6am to 8pm by soldiers and anyone wanting to use it would be made to crawl on all fours for the entire length (about 137 metres), an uncomfortable and humiliating experience. In the end, the soldiers on duty at Kucha Kurnchhan actually made natives crawl on their bellies, kicking and poking anyone who wasn't fully prostrate. The first natives to travel along in this fashion were eleven people Dyer had arrested for failing to *salaam* to him, who were apparently there by 'chance'. In total, forty-three people crawled through that street, although in an act of subversive mockery one man did it three times and had to be stopped.

The order effectively closed the street and was particularly problematic for the residents, some of whom had actually saved Miss Sherwood, hiding her until the threat had passed and taking her to safety when the coast was clear. The houses along this street had no back doors, so inhabitants were forced to sleep elsewhere so they could get to work, doctors could not visit the sick and rubbish and sewage was not taken away. Dyer also went on to publicly flog the six young men suspected (but not convicted) of the attack on the missionary – in front of the street itself. O'Dwyer cancelled the Crawling Order after he heard about it, which was around 24 to 26 April, despite having visited Amritsar on the 20th, when it was put in place but he had not been informed at the time. When O'Dwyer later questioned Dyer about it, the general concocted a story suggesting that it was an effective outlet for angry and insulted British troops who might otherwise take matters in to their own hands. There were also comments made at the Hunter Committee that suggested many did not agree with Dyer's irregular choice of retribution.

With Amritsar quiet, Dyer was told to begin a round of visits to the rural Sikh areas close to the city. Columns were sent out with the task of quelling rumours that the Golden Temple had been bombed, women raped and that the British were struggling to retain control. The tours of surrounding countryside also enabled the military to arrest anyone suspected of supporting or organising rebellion and agitation or in possession of goods obtained through lootings in Amritsar. Most of these arrests were achieved through the use of informers. During this time, Dyer occasionally faced questions from superiors and other VIPs over the massacre, but none of those enquiries were to give him a difficult time. More troops were also being sent to the city, increasing the military presence significantly. Police corruption remained an ongoing problem, but the population was clearly too scared to make a fuss over it.

More orders were being created under martial law also, despite the lack of any more uprisings – these included rules that effectively made *hartals* illegal and prevented Indians from travelling by train. *Lathis* were also banned and walking more than two abreast was forbidden. All bicycles were requisitioned for army use. Worries surfaced that Indian troops might be targeted for subversion but they proved to be groundless – even when C.F. Andrews, Gandhi's aide and confident, was deported when he visited Amritsar, there was no further trouble or protest. Dyer continued to parade through the city, pleased to see that the inhabitants were now suitably subservient. With the leaders of political opposition imprisoned, there was no appetite for rebellion. After a concerted effort to favour the Sikh section of society, Dyer and Briggs were made honorary Sikhs in a ceremony at the Golden Temple.

In the end, Amritsar lived under martial law as a result of the massacre until June. In that time, the Lahore courts saw 298 people charged with major offences and convicted 218 of them. Penalties handed down for these crimes were harsh and included death, transportation and prison sentences – some as long as ten years. The leaders of the Rowlatt agitation were singled out for particularly severe punishment, with Dr Kitchlew and Dr Satya Pal being sentenced to life transportation to the Andaman Islands. One of the organisers of the Jallianwala Bagh meeting, Dr Muhammad Bashir, was sentenced to death and forfeiture of all his property. These verdicts were reviewed however, and instead Kitchlew and Satya Pal received two years in prison, and Bashir six. The Amritsar martial law courts dealt with twenty-two cases of minor crime and tried 143 people, while the military magistrates court dealt with twenty-six cases and the military courts convicted fifty people, just over half of whom were whipped, mostly in private. The city was beaten.

By 7 May, Dyer knew that his brigade was to become part of the Afghan Field Force and handed over responsibility for Amritsar. As he waited for orders to depart to his new post, reports from his wife and niece paint a picture of a man suffering from stress, unable to sleep properly or forget what he had witnessed. If he was considering how he would explain the massacre, he was fortunate to have plenty of time to do so before questions were raised. In Amritsar and its surrounds, martial law meant critics had been effectively silenced. The local press was heavily censored, with the Editor of the *Tribune* sentenced to two years in prison and the paper suspended. It was a similar story for the *Bombay Chronicle*, where the editor – who was also a supporter of Gandhi – was deported and a reporter jailed. Gandhi became less vocal as he found he lost support for the campaign of passive resistance, which had resulted in the most violent of fallouts.

Slowly, details of the massacre did begin to circulate, which must have taken a lot of bravery on the part of the political opposition. The All India Congress Committee campaigned for an end to the emergency powers, condemned the events at Amritsar and demanded an enquiry into the measures taken in the Punjab. It also sent Indian legislator

Vitthalbai Patel and lawyer N.C. Kelkar to England to question Edwin Montagu, in his role as Secretary of State for India. The Labour Party in Britain also voiced objections and, working with Indian nationalist Bal Gangadhar (B.G.) Tilak, called for an end to martial law and an investigation. The opposition also worked with the Indian Committee of the Workers Welfare League of India to organize a meeting in Hyde Park where leaflets by prominent socialists Robert Williams, Robert Smilie and George Lansbury entitled 'Coercion, Repression and Butchery in India' were handed out. The organisers claimed a crowd of 300,000 attended, although that has never been verified.

Founder of the Indian Home Rule League, B.G. Tilak also spoke at Westminster's Caxton Hall to the British and India Society in early May on the topic – doubtless one of the many reasons he was dubbed 'father of the Indian unrest' by colonial powers. The left wing Fabian Society also played host to London Indians for a talk by Tilak and Liberal MP Commander Joseph Kenworthy (who was to later join the Labour party). Much of this commentary was not only related to Amritsar but to the general approach in the Punjab but it's clear that many were questioning the events in Jallianwala Bagh. On 1 May, Montagu told the Viceroy that an enquiry was essential; it was not just the opposition who felt that way. While the Government of India fought for the process to be internally managed – and managed to delay the start of it at least – an enquiry was inevitable. The Raj had however had the sense to rush through an Indemnity Bill that protected from prosecution those acting under martial law.

Whether or not Dyer was aware of growing concern about the behaviour of the military in India is not known, but even while he was posted to Kohat, he continued to express anxiety about his future. When he received orders for an advance on Afghan troops from Commander-in-Chief of the Northern Army, Sir Arthur Barrett, he brought up Amritsar too, seeking reassurance from his superior that he was not going to be in trouble. Barrett was General Beynon's superior officer, and therefore Dyer's second reporting officer; fortunately for Dyer, he shared his views on Indians and the disturbances in the Punjab. Unbelievably, Barrett was actually in favour of a collective financial penalty being extracted from rebellious towns such as Amritsar, charging the rich residents a fee because they did not prevent the outbreak of insurgency. It is hard to believe that he could really have thought that was necessary, as Amritsar had already paid such a high price for daring to debate the Rowlatt Act. Clearly Dyer was not alone in his views that the military did what was necessary in the Punjab, whatever the cost.

Fortunately perhaps for Dyer, his campaign in Thal proved to be a triumph and he demonstrated his worth as a strategic and dedicated military leader. Despite this, the conditions had taken a physical toll on him and when he returned he was given ten days sick leave, which he took in the cooler hills of Dalhousie. During this time, Dyer may have had the chance to catch up on current events and will have probably seen that the press was full of stories about the unrest in the Punjab. Partly recovered, in mid-July he went to rejoin his brigade in Nowshera, only to find a letter from the Adjutant-General, Lieutenant General Sir Havelock Hudson, ordering a full report on the events in Amritsar. This was the first sign that Dyer might have to explain himself and his letter was one of several that had gone out as part of initial investigations. Dyer did not keep a diary of the events to refer to, although Briggs did have log sheets of the events as they happened. Many of the people involved at the time had taken leave or were now posted elsewhere, while Irving had returned to England.

The events in the Punjab and the shooting at the Jallianwala Bagh were beginning to make waves both in India and England. The press back in London initially viewed O'Dwyer and Dyer as heroes for nipping in the bud a new wave of revolution akin to that of the Mutiny. The British in India also lauded the hardline approach to the natives and believed it had spared them from violence that was ready to sweep across the region and out into the territory as a whole. The Indian take on martial law and Amritsar was not as charitable. The native newspapers thought the punitive measures of dealing with political opposition – and in particular actions such as the Crawling Order – revealed that the British remained as racially prejudiced as ever and would never truly consider equal power sharing. The direct result of the furore was the breakdown in the relationship between the Raj and its subjects, and because of this, O'Dwyer and Dyer were not the 'saviours' of British India but in fact the ruin of it.

As word trickled out about Amritsar, the response to disturbances in the Punjab and consequent censorship and removal of civil liberties under martial law, Indians began to find ways to draw wider attention to what was happening. The Bengali Sir Rabindranath Tagore, who in 1913 became the first non-European to win the Nobel Prize for Literature, and was renowned for re-shaping regional literature, music and Indian art in the late nineteenth and early twentieth centuries, surrendered his knighthood, given to him by George V in 1915. In a letter to Chelmsford, Tagore wrote, 'the time has come when badges of honour make our shame glaring in the incongruous context of humiliation, and I for my part wish to stand, shorn of all special distinctions, by the side of those of my countrymen, who, for their so-called insignificance, are liable to suffer degradation not fit for human beings.'

Gandhi demanded a Royal Commission of Inquiry badgering both the Government of India and Edwin Montagu in London. The All India Congress Committee passed a resolution demanding an inquiry. Sir Chettur Sankaran Nair, who had been a lawyer and high court judge, resigned from the Viceroy's Executive Council and then went to London to lobby for that inquiry on behalf of Congress. Politician and founder of Varanasi University, Pandit Madan Mohan Malaviya, and missionary and reformer Swami Sharaddhanand, collected and circulated witness accounts of the Amritsar shooting. Punjab Legislative Council members Nawab Din Murad and Kartar Singh, described the massacre as 'neither just nor humane'.

There was also criticism from the Anglican priest Charles Freer Andrews, who was a friend of Gandhi. He described the massacre as 'cold-blooded and inhumane'. British journalist and editor of the *Bombay Chronicle*, B.G. Horniman managed to smuggle photographs of the incident out and broke the story about the massacre and its aftermath in the *Daily Herald*. The exposé then unleashed a wave of belated revulsion in the British. One of his correspondents, Goverdhan Das, was imprisoned for three years, while Horniman was arrested for his coverage and deported to London, causing the *Chronicle* to temporarily shut. While in England, he continued his crusade against the colonial government, returning to India a few years later to resume his editorship. Of the massacre, Horniman said, 'No event within living memory, probably, has made so deep and painful impression on the mind of the public in this country [England] as what came to be known as the Amritsar massacre.'

While the Government of India held on to its unwavering belief that its servants and its soldiers had foiled an organised rebellion hell bent on its downfall, it began to begrudgingly accept that an investigation was inevitable. On 11 June 1919, the India Office, the British government department created to oversee the administration of the Provinces of British India, asked the Government of India to submit proposals for how an inquiry might look. Edwin Montagu was, to begin with, more concerned about the restrictions of martial law in the colony as he had only had the barest of facts presented to him regarding Amritsar at this point, with the estimated 200 'casualties' proving to be not only incredibly conservative but also somewhat of a euphemism for slaughtered Indians. When the true nature of Jallianwala Bagh was revealed, more and more British in England were appalled. Churchill, in his speech in Parliament called the massacre 'an episode which appears to me to be without precedent or parallel in the modern history of the British Empire'.

In fact, O'Dwyer had given Montagu the impression that Dyer fired on the crowd because he was afraid of an attack on his men, but this version of events skirted around two key issues – the fact that Dyer gave no warning he would give the order to shoot and that the dead and injured were left where they fell. Montagu had been horrified to learn about the Crawling Order Dyer had imposed in Amritsar and telegraphed Lord Chelmsford to say Dyer should be relieved of his command. But the Viceroy did not agree. He defended Dyer's military credentials by referencing the recent campaign in Thal and, despite not visiting Amritsar or the Punjab region himself, felt satisfied that Dyer should stay in command. Montagu did not push the matter, a move he would probably come to regret, as by saying nothing he probably felt guilty by association.

And the Viceroy wasn't Dyer's only supporter. The Commander-in-Chief of India, General Sir Charles Monro, congratulated Dyer on his time in Thal when Dyer was called to Simla. The Adjutant General, Lieutenant General Sir Havelock Hudson, was also happy to defend Dyer at this point, as was the Quartermaster-General, Lieutenant General Sir George Fletcher Macmunn. Dyer clearly had the support of every officer superior to him. But these were military men, from the same army culture as Dyer. Dyer didn't get as warm a welcome when he met Sir William Vincent, the Home Member of the Viceroy's council, and the most senior civil servant in the Government of India. This was a civilian, perhaps of a different mindset to a lifelong soldier who had an almost institutionalised disdain for both natives and civilians.

Vincent was apparently stunned by Dyer's confidence and insistence that he had saved the Punjab. Vincent was shrewd enough to see the holes in the way the Amritsar massacre had been presented by its instigators so far. He realised the 'fear of being overwhelmed' didn't account for the length of time that Dyer's men continued to fire for, or the need for Dyer to instruct his men to aim for certain areas of the crowd. It also didn't help that Dyer maintained that if he had had more ammunition, he would have continued to order his men to shoot for still longer. This story also contradicted the reports that Dyer offered at other times, when he said he knew a crowd had gathered despite his proclamation banning such activities. Still only partly recovered, after his visit to Simla, Dyer returned again to Dalhousie to escape the heat.

Back in England, pressure to investigate the state of affairs in India increased. The House of Lords debated the issue and Earl Russell objected to the death sentence that had been handed to influential businessman Lala Harkishen Lal under martial law for his part in anti-Rowlatt Bill agitation. But others were keen to exaggerate the level of rebellion, to excuse the way the government of India was dealing with internal issues. Lord Sydenham, who was known to support O'Dwyer's approach, made much of the attack on Miss Sherwood and referenced the Mutiny and anti-British feelings. The Indian peer, Lord Satyendra Sinha, who was the Under-Secretary of State for India – and the highest-ranking Indian in the British government at the time – spoke but did not raise the matter of the shooting at Amritsar.

By 25 August, still convalescing, Dyer finished the first official report on his actions at Amritsar, a mere four months after it had happened. It was full of personal opinions and justifications for the shooting – and different from the 14 April report and explanations he had previously given to Wathen, Irving, O'Dwyer and Beynon. It was five pages long – with a staggering twenty-six-pages of appendixes – and was supported by letters from two British clergymen that backed up the claim that this one event prevented violence from engulfing the region. The terms mutineers, mutiny and mutinous were used over and over again, presumably to capture the imagination of the reader and bring flooding back unsettling memories of previous unrest and bloodshed.

Within the report, Dyer makes much of his motivation and personal experience in similar circumstances. He also mentions the unrest he witnessed in Delhi, explains he had held fire on the 12th and that the shooting was not just designed to disperse the crowd but to provide a 'moral effect' that he wanted to take hold across the whole of the Punjab. He describes his own proclamation procession, claims he heard that rebels were meeting and on seeing the crowd in Jallianwala Bagh saw it was the same group of people who had started the violence in the city on the 10th. He claims that there was no need to issue a warning that he would fire on the gathering, because those there were familiar with his proclamation. He also adds that tending to the wounded may have left his force vulnerable to an attack that they did not have the firepower left to deal with. This report made it clear that there was no warning and that the sustained firing was designed not to clear the area in this instance but to prevent further rebellion. There was no mention of the fact that he fired as a response to feeling his troops might be overwhelmed or that he was unaware that the crowd was effectively trapped in the Bagh – although these had been key elements of the story he had told his superior officers – and facts that they had accepted. Dyer sent his report to the Hunter Committee.

Of course, it's hard to know the real truth about Dyer's motivation for firing and how he handled the men under his command in the heat of the moment; did he change his version of events – or did he finally tell the truth? What is clear is that Dyer assembled men that were equipped to fire and that he took none of the company commanders with him, and so did not seek any advice on alternate actions at the time. He also had time to consider his response to the gathering he had forbidden and intelligence on the size of the crowd gathered both by the police and by spotter plane.

Dyer was probably quite confident that he was covered by his report however, returning on a high from his successful campaign in Thal, having had all his superior officers previously voice their support for him and having read the London press calling him a hero. Further support for him came in General Beynon's official report, completed in early September, that stated that since Dyer's actions in Amritsar there had been no further trouble in the city or in Lahore and that Dyer had since rebuilt a relationship with the local Sikh community. At this point in time, Beynon was also recommending Dyer for an award following his campaign against the Afghan forces, placing Dyer in line for a CBE. The Adjutant General, Lieutenant General Sir Havelock Hudson also defended Dyer and even his Crawling Order.

In the wider arena, during September, the Imperial Legislative Council was discussing the Indemnity Bill – designed to protect those that had acted to restore order under martial law from prosecution or punishment. While Indian members such as former Congress President Pandit Madan Malaviya, understandably wanted to raise the issue of how the Punjab disturbances had been handled, the government and the Council pushed the Bill through, regardless of full support. From this approach, it's clear that the government was preparing to back Dyer – and anyone like him who might also be criticised after the upcoming inquiry.

The Indian National Congress mounted its own inquiry in October 1919, no doubt fearing that the Anglo-organised one might not be entirely free from bias. Many notable and educated Indians, including Pandit Motilal, Bengali nationalist, C.R. Das, Swami Sharaddhanand, C.F. Andrews, Jawarhalal Nehru and Puru Shottam Das Tandon, organised the Inquiry. Gandhi was also part of the committee once the order banning him from the Punjab expired. The Congress Inquiry gathered an immense amount of witness statements, finally giving a voice to the victims of the Jallianwala Bagh shooting, rather than just the officials who ordered or sanctioned it. During this Inquiry, Gandhi came into his own, putting his legal skills to good use, interviewing witnesses, meticulously recording statements and preparing evidence that would stand up to rigorous examination in law courts. His work here, and the friendships he made with other nationalists, changed Gandhi's outlook on the British Raj forever. Horrified at the cruel and oppressive way in which some of the British treated Indian natives, Gandhi became opposed to any form of British Rule in the continent. The events at Amritsar effectively turned one of India's most charismatic leaders and the peaceful protestor into an ardent supporter of freedom from the Empire.

On 14 October, the Government of India published Resolution 2168, which announced an Inquiry into the disturbances in Bombay, Delhi and the Punjab. It was expected to examine both the causes of the rebellion and the measures taken to counter it. The Hunter Committee would certainly go down in history.

BOMBAY on the Malabar Coast, belonging to the East India Company of ENGLAND.

Bombay circa 1745 when the city was the property of the East India company. (*Mary Evans Picture Library*)

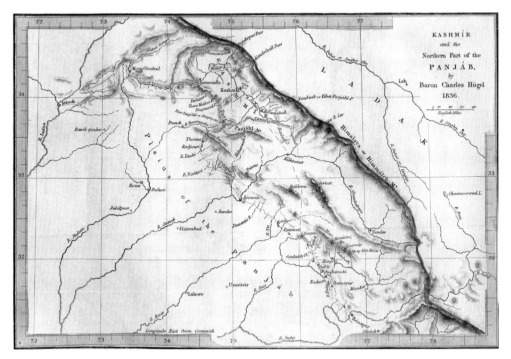

Map of the Punjab dated 1836. (© *Antiquarian Images/Mary Evans*)

Left: The execution of sepoy mutineers in 1857. (*Mary Evans/Everett Collection*)

Below: Lord Curzon who served as Viceroy of India from 1899 to 1905. (*Mary Evans Picture Library*)

Maharajah of Rewa   Lord Curzon   Captain Wigram, A.D.C.

LORD CURZON OF KEDLESTON IN THE JUNGLE AND HIS BAG OF TIGERS

THE NEW LIBERAL GOVERNMENT: MEMBERS OF THE CABINET.

Mr. H. Gladstone.   Mr. Haldane.   Mr. Sydney Buxton.   Earl Carrington.   Lord Tweedmouth.
    Earl of Crewe.   Mr. Bryce.   Mr. Lloyd-George.   Sir H. Fowler.   Mr. Augustine Birrell.   Mr. J. Sinclair

Sir H. Campbell-Bannerman.
Sir R. Reid.   Sir E. Grey.   Earl of Elgin.   Mr. Morley.   Marquis of Ripon.   Mr. Asquith.   Mr. John Burns.

The cabinet of the 1905 Liberal Government, including reformist John Morley. (*Mary Evans/Pharcide*)

Simla, Punjab Government House

Government House in Simla, the summer capital of the Raj and boyhood home of Reginald Dyer. (*Mary Evans Picture Library*)

By the passing of the Indian Councils Act, 1909, the constitution of the Governor-General's Legislative Council has been materially modified. The Act is entitled "An Act to Amend the Indian Councils Acts, 1861 and 1892, and the Government of India Act, 1833, (25th May, 1909.)

Section 1 provides that "The additional members of the councils for the purpose of making laws and regulations (hereinafter referred to as legislative councils) of the Governor-General and of the governors of Fort Saint George and Bombay and the members of the legislative councils already constituted or which may hereafter be constituted of the several lieutenant-governors of provinces, instead of being all nominated by the Govenor-General, governor, or lieutenant-governor, in manner provided by the Indian Councils Acts, 1861 and 1892, shall include members so nominated and also members elected in accordance with regulations made under this Act."

FIRST SCHEDULE OF THE INDIAN COUNCILS ACT

Maximum numbers of nominated and elected members of Legislative Councils

Legislative Council	Maximum Number
Legislative Council of the Governor-General	60
Legislative Council of the Governor of Fort St. George	50
Legislative Council of the Governor of Bombay	50

Above: The Legislative Council of India c. 1910, Lord Minto is seated at the centre. (© *Illustrated London News Ltd/ Mary Evans*)

Left: British colonial life c. 1918, an elephant excursion. (*Mary Evans Picture Library/ Margaret Monck*)

Right: Viceroy Lord Chelmsford in 1919, with the Maharaja of Kapurthala (right). (*Mary Evans Picture Library/ Margaret Monck)*

Below: The golden viceregal coach used for state occasions in India c.1920. (*Mary Evans Picture Library/ Margaret Monck*)

Left: Mohandas Karamchand Gandhi
c. 1900 aged 30 when he was working
in South Africa. (*Mary Evans/Everett
Collection*)

Below: Gandhi many years later, spinning
cloth and wearing traditional dress.
(*Mary Evans Picture Library*)

Gandhi il *Tessitore*.

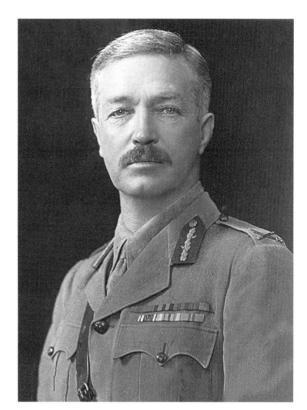

Right: Brigadier General
R.E.H. Dyer in 1920.
(*Public domain*)

Below: The Jallianwala Bagh
where the massacre took place.
(*Public domain*)

Above: The Golden Temple in Amritsar, a pilgrimage site for the Sikh religion. (*Photo by Ravi Jha on Unsplash*)

Left: Winston Churchill in the army, 1915. Churchill would go on to condemn Dyer's actions at Amritsar. (*Mary Evans Picture Library*)

BACK TO THE ARMY AGAIN: MR. CHURCHILL AND HIS NEW CHIEF

The political event of the week has been Mr. Churchill's resignation, followed by his personal statement in the House of Commons. "I feel unable, in times like these, to remain in well-paid inactivity; I therefore ask you to submit my resignation to the King." Mr. Churchill wrote to the Prime Minister. "I am an officer, and I place myself unreservedly at the disposal of the military authorities, observing that my regiment is in France."

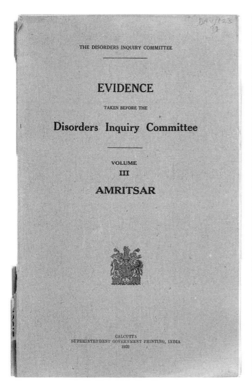

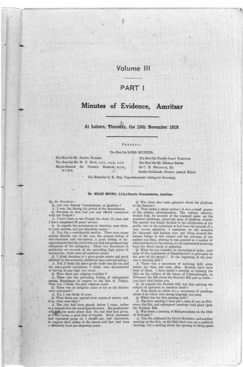

Above left and right: Minutes of Evidence taken before the Hunter Committee. (*Parliamentary Information licensed under the Open Parliament Licence v.3.0.*)

Right: The 1940 assassination of Sir Michael O'Dwyer by Udham Singh, who blamed the former Lieutenant Governor of the Punjab for the massacre. (© *John Frost Newspapers/ Mary Evans Picture Library*)

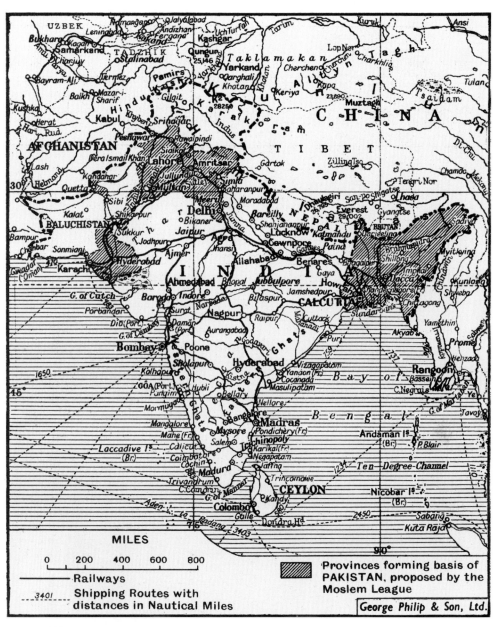

A map showing the proposed partition of India and Pakistan. (© *Illustrated London News Ltd/Mary Evans*)

MR. EDWIN MONTAGU'S INDIAN BOMBSHELL
THE MINISTER'S RESIGNATION AND GANDHI'S ARREST

MR. MONTAGU DRIVING HIS—

—ARGUMENTS HOME AT CAMBRIDGE

THE THREE ACTS OF THE STORY

Act 1.—March 9.—Lord Reading on behalf of Indian Government.

On the eve of the Greco-Turkish Conference we feel it our duty again to lay before his Majesty's Government the intensity of feeling in India regarding the necessity for a revision of the Sevres Treaty. The Government of India are fully alive to the complexity of the problem, but India's services in the war, in which Indian Moslem soldiers so largely participated, and the support which the Indian Moslem cause is receiving throughout India, entitle her to claim the utmost fulfilment of her just and equitable aspirations. The Government of India particularly urge, subject to the safeguarding of the neutrality of the Straits and of the security of the non-Moslem population, the following three points, namely:—

The evacuation of Constantinople,
The suzerainty of the Sultan over the Holy places, and
The restoration of Ottoman Thrace (including Adrianople) and Smyrna.
The fulfilment of these three points is of the greatest importance to India.

Act 2.—March 10.—Mr. Chamberlain in the House of Commons.

I understand this telegram was published by the Government of India with the sanction of the Secretary of State. No other Minister was consulted. . . . His Majesty's Government are unable to reconcile the publication of the telegram of the Government of India on the sole responsibility of the Secretary of State with the collective responsibility of the Cabinet or with the duty which all the Governments of the Empire owe to each other in matters of Imperial concern. Such independent declarations destroy the unity of policy, which it is vital to preserve in foreign affairs.

Act 3.—March 11.—Mr. Edwin Montagu at Cambridge.

It is said that I have outraged the doctrine of collective Cabinet responsibility. I do not think I have. Accusation of a breach of the doctrine of responsibility from the Prime Minister of all men in the world is a laughable accusation. The head of the Government is a Prime Minister of great, if eccentric, genius. He has demanded the price which it is in the power of every genius to demand, and that price has been the complete disappearance of Cabinet responsibility. Cabinet responsibility is a joke—a pretext. We have been governed by a dictator. The real reason is the " Die-hard " party's dislike of me. The Prime Minister has done for them what they could not do for themselves, and to get their support, for which Lord Birkenhead pleaded, he has presented them with my head upon a charger.

THE EARL OF READING
who, as Viceroy, sent the message published.

MR. M. K. GANDHI
the agitator, who has been arrested.

A MORE PLEASANT PHASE OF LIFE IN INDIA : INCIDENTS DURING THE PRINCE'S VISIT TO DELHI

Presenting the King's medal to a Delhi police inspector.   Talking with the wives of the N.C.O.s of the Seaforths.   Presenting cup to winner in tent-pegging competition.

Edwin Montagu resigns as Secretary of State for India over British policy in Turkey.

Above: The Jallianwala Bagh memorial today. (*Adobe Stock*)

Left: Bullet marks in the walls at Jallianwala Bagh. (*Adobe Stock*)

Today signs at the Jallianwala Bagh show where bullets marked the walls. (*Adobe Stock*)

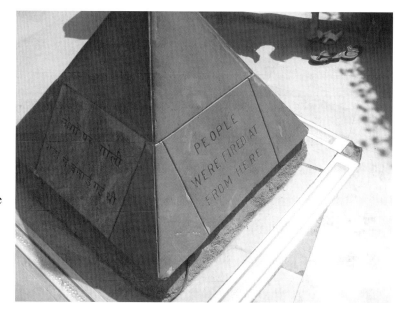

A stone marks where soldiers took aim at the crowds. (*Photo by tjollans on flickr*)

The original walls of the Jallianwala Bagh show the walls sprayed with bullet marks. (*Photo by Stefan Krasowski on flickr*)

The Martyrs Well at Jallianwala Bagh, where many died as they sought refuge. (*Photo by Dinesh Bareja on flickr*)

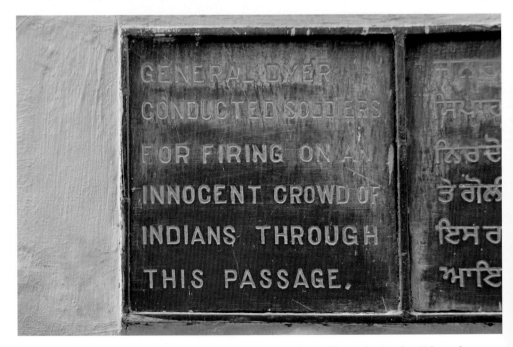

Signage on the narrow streets that approach the Jallianwala Bagh. (*Photo by Shanker S. on flickr*)

की उपस्थिति में 13 अप्रैल, 1961 को किया गया।

JALLIANWALA BAGH

JALLIANWALA BAGH MASSACRE INVOLVED THE KILLING OF HUNDREDS OF UNARMED, DEFENSELESS INDIANS BY A SENIOR BRITISH MILITARY OFFICER, BRIGADIER -GENERAL REGINALD EDWARD HARRY DYER ON 13TH APRIL, 1919 AT THIS SPOT, IN THE HOLY CITY OF AMRITSAR. THE JALIANWALA BAGH THEN WAS PROPERTY OF FAMILY OF SARDAR HIMMAT SINGH, A NOBLE IN THE COURT OF MAHARAJA RANJIT SINGH. GENERAL DYER DEPLOYED HIS RIFFLE MEN, NEAR THE ENTRANCE AND WITHOUT WARNING OR ORDER THE CROWD TO DISPERSE, OPENED FIRE. THE FIRING CONTINUED FOR 20 MINUTES AND 1650 ROUNDS OF 0.303 MARK VI AMMUNITION HAD BEEN FIRED. THE OFFICIAL FIGURE IS 379 KILLED AND 1,200 WOUNDED. THE CROWD WAS ESTIMATED AT BETWEEN 15,000 AND 20,000. THE JALLIANWALA BAGH WAS ACQUIRED BY THE NATION ON 1ST AUGUST 1920 AT THE COST OF RS. 5.65/- LAKHS AND THE MEMORIAL BEFITTINGLY NAMED "THE FLAME OF LIBERTY" WAS BUILT AT A COST OF RS. 9.25/- LAKHS. IT WAS INAUGURATED BY DR. RAJINDER PRASAD, THE FIRST PRESIDENT OF REPUBLIC INDIA IN THE PRESENCE OF PT. JAWAHAR LAL NEHRU, FIRST PRIME MINISTER OF INDIA ON 13th APRIL, 1961.

ਜਲ੍ਹਿਆਂਵਾਲਾ ਬਾਗ

The details of the Jallianwala Bagh continue to shock today. (*Photo by Shanker S. on flickr*)

David Cameron laid a wreath at the Jallianwala Bagh in 2013 but did not offer an official apology. (*Shutterstock/EPA*)

Above: London Mayor Sadiq Khan stands in silence after laying a wreath at the Jallianwala Bagh memorial in 2017. (*Shutterstock/EPA-EFE*)

Left: Virendra Sharma MP for Ealing Southall, who is campaigning for all aspects of colonial history to be taught in British schools, a permanent memorial for the Jallianwala Bagh victims and an official apology. (*With thanks to the office of Virendra Sharma MP*)

Chapter 8

The Hunter Committee

The Hunter Committee – as it came to be known – was chaired by Lord William Hunter, who had been Scotland's Solicitor General under the Liberal Asquith government and was a Member of Parliament for Glasgow Govan from 1910 to 1911. In December 1911, Hunter was appointed a Senator of the College of Justice, the legal institution that administers justice in Scotland, when he took the judicial title Lord, and sat on the bench until 1936. He had no connection – and therefore no experience of, or romantic affection for – British India. No doubt this displeased many who felt that to understand what motivated the government of India and the Indian Army to act as they did during the political struggles and disturbances there required a 'certain type'. Of course, it also meant that he was less likely to have any preconceived notions about 'the natives' or the innate superiority of their British rulers. The investigation was officially referred to as the Disorders Inquiry Committee, and its first meeting took place on 29 October 1919.

Montagu achieved a commendable balance within the board, including a range of experience both legal and military; along with Lord Hunter, there were a further four British and three Indian members, appointing H.G. Stokes, Secretary to the Government of Madras, as Committee Secretary. The other members were W.F. Rice, Additional Secretary to the Government of India at the Home Department; Justice G.C. Rankin, Judge of the High Court, Calcutta; Major General Sir George Barrow, Commandant of the Peshawar Division; Thomas Smith, a member of the Legislative Council of the United Provinces; Sir Chimanlal Setalvad, an eminent Indian barrister and jurist; Pandit Jagat Narayan, another lawyer and also a member of the Legislative Council of the United Provinces; and Sardar Sultan Ahmed Khan, Member for Appeals for Gwalior State.

At the first meeting, the Committee was presented with evidence gathered only by the government of India, leaving it open to the entirely reasonable criticism that the information it was working with was very much one-sided. The material collected by the Indian government did not include statements from anyone currently held in prison for the uprising, any opponents of the Raj or anyone from the general population in the areas affected by martial law, the massacre or its fallout. It was simply the collected views of civil servants and military officers, information controlled by the government of India.

Such was the lack of confidence in the material which the Hunter Committee examined that the Indian National Congress boycotted the enquiry after 19 November, instead setting up its own non-official committee. On the Congress committee sat Motilal Nehru, a lawyer and politician, who was to become the president of the Amritsar Congress in December; Chittaranjan (C.R.) Das, a leading politician, lawyer, activist and founder-leader of the Swaraj Party in Bengal; Abbas Tyabji, a wealthy, British-educated Muslim from Gujarat and Chief Justice of Baroda State; and M.R. Jayakar, called to the Bar in London and the first Vice-Chancellor of the University of Poona and Gandhi. These men were well educated, with knowledge of the judicial system, and several had been sympathetic to the Raj in the past. Their support for British rule, in light of the way the political opposition was dealt with however, had started to wane.

Another aspect of the Hunter Commission that was heavily criticised was the way in which the witnesses, called from Delhi, Lahore, Ahmedabad and Bombay, were to testify. The majority of those questioned were not placed under oath and had to give their evidence in public. Effectively, this meant that there was no confidentiality afforded to anyone that wished to become a whistleblower and that they were not legally obliged to tell the truth in the same way as they would be in a criminal court. The witnesses were however questioned thoroughly and at length, as the Committee had the advantage of professionals skilled at picking apart a story for anomalies. Some of those giving evidence did complain about the cross-examinations they received – not least O'Dwyer, who was no doubt enraged that Indian members of the committee were able to address him in such a way. The officers and civil servants present were used to being held in a position of respect by natives and the public and also to being above having to explain themselves to those that they did not consider their equal.

By the time the Committee came to interview Dyer, it was well practiced in its unrelenting interviewing style. The events at the Jallianwala Bagh and Dyer's Crawling Order were important aspects of the investigation and prior to Dyer's time before the Committee it had gathered much information about them. Dyer appeared in Lahore before the Hunter Commission on 19 November for a full day, during which every member of the committee questioned him. Dyer had several disadvantages. Firstly, he had none of the supporting evidence he had expected from his friend Briggs, who had unfortunately been taken into hospital with appendicitis on the day Dyer went before the committee and was to die the next day. Secondly, he had refused the help of a legal council, his evidence being given in a rowdy public hall. Dyer was later to dispute some of what was recorded and it does seem that the minutes were taken in an unorthodox fashion.

During the inquiry, Dyer probably answered the questions a little too honestly for his own good. He admitted that not everyone in the Jallianwala Bagh crowd would have been aware of the proclamation, that he might have been able to disperse the crowd without firing, that he continued firing to make an impression – and also because he didn't want anyone laughing at him – and that because he knew the meeting was scheduled at the Bagh he could have prevented people from entering. He also explained that he instigated the Crawling Order to reinforce the sacredness of women, that he thought public floggings made more of an impression than those carried out behind closed doors and that he went to Jallianwala Bagh with the intention of firing on the crowd, and 'firing well'. He also concurred that if the armoured cars he had at his disposal had fitted down the narrow city streets of Amritsar, he would have sent them into the Bagh and used the mounted machine guns, causing even more deaths.

Dyer also stood by his contentious claim that he fired to strike terror and reduce the morale of rebels across the Punjab, punishing the crowd at Amritsar to serve as a lesson elsewhere. It was during the Hunter Commission that Dyer explained this action as his 'horrible duty', because he knew by punishing the dissenters it would make an impression across the Punjab and that his actions would be a justifiable way to prevent further bloodshed. This version of events contradicted his first accounts in which he claimed he was worried that the crowd at the Jallianwala Bagh would overcome his small force, and that caused him to open fire. But it fitted in with the role of the 'Saviour of India' that he now cast himself in. He agreed that he saw the Rowlatt agitation as a rebellion and admitted he had left the wounded, as it was not his job to deal with them and the hospitals were open.

The Inquiry must have been quite an ordeal for Dyer. He was ill, the crowd was hostile and the panel consisted of accomplished interviewers, skilled in leading a witness. It's clear that there was some bias to some of the questions and Dyer was either stupid or arrogant enough to speak freely, even if that meant incriminating himself. But perhaps that also shows how confident he was that his deeds would not only go unpunished but would be applauded. Both O'Dwyer and General Beynon felt that Dyer had been goaded into many of the answers he gave, but Dyer stuck with this version of events as they appeared within his report filed on 25 August. The details did however clash with what he told Wathen, Irving, Sir Edward Douglas Maclagan (the Lieutenant General who replaced O'Dwyer), Hailey, Beynon, and O'Dwyer, who later admitted what Dyer said to the Hunter Committee was 'indefensible' but was the result of the way he had been questioned.

Dyer's evidence at the Inquiry was to be his downfall; his behaviour had clearly broken rules and protocol. Despite this, Dyer apparently remained upbeat after he had given his evidence, perhaps because both Beynon and Maclagan had made their support for him clear. The members of the Hunter Commission however were not in such accord, with the Indian members reportedly refusing completely to speak to Lord Hunter by the end of proceedings. The truth was, it was impossible for those loyal to the Empire to accept that Dyer was in the wrong, and it was inconceivable to those fighting for Indian equality to see the actions by the British in the Punjab as anything but racist and as an illustration that self-governance would never be accepted.

Because the Inquiry was open to the public, events were soon reported in the media. The Indian press was first to publish with the London papers hot on their heels. The Indian National Congress sent its evidence to its British committee, which was able to release a report there. The *Daily Express* broke the story in England on 13 December and made much of the numbers reportedly killed; at the trial estimates of four to five hundred dead were given. The figures appeared again two days later in *The Times*. These reports alerted Edwin Montagu to the fact he had been misled over the incident and how he had in some way, even unknowingly, been complicit in keeping the massacre quiet. He telegraphed the Viceroy asking him to explain the discrepancy between the figures reported at the Hunter Commission and the smaller one he had been told, and in turn reported to the Commons. Five days later, after he'd been grilled over the incident in the House, Montagu was still chasing an answer from the Viceroy.

While Montagu had to use the excuse that he was waiting for the findings of the Hunter Inquiry before fully discussing the matter, it must have been clear to him that, by not providing him with the full information ahead of the press getting hold of the story, Chelmsford had left him out on a limb. It is also thought that Montagu immediately saw the significance of what Dyer had done – knew that it was a tragedy that would have far-reaching implications – and worried that he could have in some way prevented it. For their part, the government of India and the Viceroy either did not recognize how the Hunter Commission's findings would be received overseas – outside of the bubble of the British Raj in India – or just didn't want to accept and deal with it. Or simply didn't care.

Now all the British papers, bar the *Morning Post*, were critical of Dyer and his actions in Amritsar. Montagu faced questions again in the House, this time from a Liberal colleague, asking if Dyer had been relieved of his command and if Montagu was in possession of any of the findings of the Inquiry yet. Of course, Montagu had been purposefully left in the dark by Viceroy Chelmsford and had no real knowledge of what had happened or what was to happen. No doubt he was beginning to feel very foolish and let down. It was now also obvious to Montagu that Dyer was still in a position of command in India and potentially able to commit more atrocities. Montagu asked the Viceroy why he hadn't suspended Dyer during the Inquiry and if he had taken any action to avoid a repeat of any of the humiliations imposed by the British under martial law. He also bemoaned the lack of information and wanted to know that Dyer would not be put in charge of any civilian disturbances.

But the Viceroy continued to hide behind the Hunter Commission, giving out as little information as he could, avoiding taking any pre-emptive action, hoping that by some miracle, the outcome of the investigation would exonerate Dyer, his superior officers and the government of India. It was an unlikely hope. The British in India also stood blindly behind Dyer; O'Dwyer even took it upon himself to wage a war of words with Montagu on his behalf, criticising Montagu's work in the House. The ongoing quarrels with O'Dwyer, and his frustration in dealing with Chelmsford, undoubtedly added to the stress that saw Montagu suffer a nervous breakdown that required him to retreat to a nursing home from January to March in 1920. Later O'Dwyer also saw fit to pass two letters he wrote to Montagu to the press in June of that year; clearly, he had no sympathy for a politician showing compassion. O'Dwyer's aims were clear – to protect himself and his colleagues and to preserve British India.

Back in London, the government could clearly see the damage the Inquiry was having. And it had the Montagu-Chelmsford reforms to implement, which needed Indian subjects to be in a loyal frame of mind. Instead, relations were at an all-time low. The natives boycotted the festivities celebrating the victory of the First World War, with a grand military procession finding the streets on its route deserted and shops shut. What could be done to repair the relationship between master and servant? Relief came when on 31 December 1919, the King Emperor announced an amnesty, offering clemency for all those arrested and imprisoned because of political offences during the recent disturbances, just as the reform act was given royal assent. This proved to be a clever move and it was well-received, putting relations back on track for a time. Even the Indian National Congress thanked George V for his clemency, as it met in late December and praised the new reforms. But Congress also mentioned the lack of condemnation for the events in the Jallianwala and passed a resolution demanding Dyer be removed from his post.

Meanwhile, Dyer had returned to his post in Jamrud, only to find his ill health meant he needed to retreat to Jullundur, where his health continued to deteriorate. He asked for six-months leave so that he could convalesce in England but was told this would only be an option if he vacated his post in 5 Brigade. Perhaps knowing he would not be offered another, Dyer carried on, but was prevented from taking up what would have been a very active role, as temporary commander of the 2nd division by his physical limitations. Instead, he found himself hospitalised, a place he would leave, not because he had recovered but because he was shortly to be summoned to his last military meeting.

Finally, by 8 March 1920, Chelmsford had the Hunter Commission report on his desk. It was an expansive document – with 200 pages of text alone – accompanied by maps and photographs and six thick volumes of evidence (two of which were classified). If that wasn't daunting enough, its contents revealed that the members of the committee had failed to reach a united verdict. Instead, the members had taken sides along racial lines, with the three Indian members of the committee failing to agree with their British colleagues and filing instead a minority report. The Inquiry had failed to bring accord even to those sitting on it and now it simply mirrored the wider feelings of British India. Instead of bringing some kind of conclusion to the events, the lack of consensus opened up more discussion and disagreements. It's easy to imagine Chelmsford's despair that this document was not the salvation he had hoped for.

True, there was some common ground reached by the two sides of the panel, as both agreed that Dyer was wrong not to issue a warning before he ordered his men to fire, that the length of firing was also an error, and that Dyer's motive to create a 'moral effect' was misguided and not in his remit. However, the minority report went further, criticising Dyer because there were innocent people in the crowd and there had been no violence at the Bagh beforehand. It argued that because some individuals in Amritsar had acted rebelliously a few days previously, it was not acceptable to assume every person in Amritsar was also intent on sedition. The two sides disagreed on Dyer leaving the wounded where they fell; the British members of the panel felt this was reasonable and had not caused unnecessary suffering, while the Indian members felt Dyer should have attended to them himself or instructed the civil authorities to do so instead. And while the majority of the Committee just disputed Dyer's claim that he had saved the Punjab from further disorder and stated there was no evidence to suggest an organised mutiny was taking place, the minority went further, arguing that Dyer had done just the opposite and actually damaged relations between sovereign and servant in British India. They were spot on.

The final majority verdict of the Hunter Report effectively let Dyer off the hook by suggesting it was more of a misunderstanding than a deliberately dreadful deed, it read:

> 'Giving all due weight to these considerations the deliberate conclusion at which we have arrived is that General Dyer exceeded the reasonable requirements of the case and showed a misconception of duty which resulted in a lamentable and unnecessary loss of life.'

It was a sentiment echoed the following year by the Army Council, which preferred to look at Dyer's actions as 'an error of judgment'.

After the Hunter Report was delivered, Dyer received his first order on 5 March to report to the commander in chief in Delhi four days later. Still in hospital however, medical staff refused to allow it, later recommending six months sick leave instead. But by 18 March, 10 days after the Hunter report had been handed over, Dyer received another order asking him to report on the 23rd, an official order immediately followed up by a personal message from the commander in chief with words to the same effect. This time, Dyer was released to attend, taking a medical officer called Captain Beamish with him. It was not to be a positive meeting, although when it was first arranged, it's unlikely a firm decision had been made on what was to pass there.

Just as it had been hard for the Hunter Committee to completely agree upon Dyer's actions and motives, the Viceroy's Legislative Council also had differing opinions on how to deal with him once the report was published. While it was clear to all that Dyer could no longer be defended, sympathy for him – or lack of it – varied across the Council. Views ranged from believing he acted wrongly, but thought he was doing the right thing, and that placing Dyer on the army's unemployed list was enough of a punishment, to asking for his retirement. Mian Sir Muhammad Shafi – the only Indian member of the Council – wanted Dyer dismissed from service, believing his actions were deliberate. Military member Lieutenant General Sir Havelock Hudson felt Dyer had made an error of judgment and was unfit for command, Sir William Vincent – the most senior civil servant on the Council – felt that Dyer should not be in his position, but that he should not be prosecuted. And Legal member Sir George Lowndes concurred it would be difficult to secure a conviction either in a civil court or via a court martial. However, the overall feeling of the Council was that Dyer had gone too far in Amritsar, and showed a lack of humanity.

Now the government of India found itself in a difficult position. If it attempted to convict Dyer to justify his forced retirement but failed, it risked native outrage if Dyer sought to be re-instated. The matter was passed to Commander in Chief of India, General Charles Carmichael Monro. Monro thought Dyer should have shown more restraint, as befitted an experienced officer, and agreed that Dyer should retire. However, he was also well aware that by punishing Dyer he ran the risk of him becoming a martyr to other servicemen, sacrificed by the politicians in return for support for a slow transition to home rule (rather than independence) from the nationalists. Monro agreed with the Hunter Commission. Dyer's recent service in Thal and his overall distinguished military career were not enough to save him.

Dyer reported to General HQ in Delhi as requested and was sent straight to Monro's office. General Hudson intercepted Dyer in the anteroom and broke the news to him that he was to be relieved of his command, asking him not to make a fuss in front of Monro. Unbelievably, Dyer agreed, was seen by Monro who told him to resign and that he would not be re-employed, and then left without even speaking. Dyer was removed from his post and put on the unemployed list on half pay. He had been judged and sentenced without a chance to defend himself and with no formal process followed, a fact his supporters made much of. Although he answered questions at the Hunter Inquiry, he was never to directly face accusations – or be able to answer them. He only saw a copy of the Hunter Committee's findings once back in England.

Dyer's fall from grace must have come as a shock for him – after all, his superior officers had previously supported him and there was no real explanation as to why or when that had changed. He returned to Jullundur only to be rushed back into hospital – with his wife also seriously ill at the time. Things must have been pretty bleak. On 24 March, he was told by letter to resign. Three days later he penned a dispatch to the General Officer Commanding 2nd Division resigning as Brigadier General Commanding the 5th Infantry Brigade. It was a sad and sorry end to a long career in which he had studied and worked hard and made many sacrifices. The humiliation was to continue as the Dyers attempted to make their way back to England, only to find that they were forbidden to travel, by an order restricting them to Jullundur issued by Sir Charles Dobell. They were prevented again when they planned to make a passage from Bombay by a meeting that was then cancelled.

When all the restrictions were lifted, the Dyers set off from Jullundur on 6 April, bound for Bombay and a passage home to England. They did at least leave knowing they had the support of the Indian regiments and local British, with their departure marked by saluting sepoys and a guard of honour formed by NCOs. Over one hundred ladies in the Punjab also signed an address expressing their gratitude. Captain Beamish escorted the couple via train to the port and then on to a hostel where they stayed for the night until boarding a hospital ship alone bound for England. A year after violence first surfaced in Amritsar, the Dyers left India, never to return. Even as they left, a crowd of supporters cheered them – but at the same time, Dyer's recommendation for an award for his time in the Afghan campaign was being cancelled.

The Report of the Disorders Enquiry Committee (India) reached London just before the Dyers set sail for England. Viceroy Chelmsford however didn't manage to send a hard copy of the report to Montagu until 16 April, along with a letter telling Montagu the Dyers were on their way home. Since this communication was sent by sea, it was only scheduled to arrive six days after the Dyers so was not at all helpful – if not downright devious. Montagu however had not waited for feedback on the findings of the Hunter Commission from the Government of India; he was fed up to the back teeth of its characteristic slow responses on the topic. The Secretary of State for India had already successfully lobbied for a committee considering the findings of the Hunter Report to be formed.

Montagu was to chair the Indian Disorders Committee, with senior government ministers making up the members. This included the Lord Chancellor, Lord Birkenhead; Edward Shortt, the Chief Secretary of Ireland; the Secretary of State for Colonies Alfred Milner; and Winston Churchill, the Secretary of State for War. Many of these ministers were also on the Cabinet Committee on the Irish situation and were thus schooled in the delicate balance of governing alongside support for nationalism. Knowing that Dyer was due home, Montagu was keen to have a plan in place before his arrival to avoid the Conservative opposition using Dyer as a pawn in their battle against reforms in India.

Montagu also knew that Dyer was very sick, had been told that the army felt his actions had been excessive and had asked for his resignation – making it clear that he would not receive another command – and that Dyer had done as requested and resigned. He had been advised that a successful conviction of Dyer was unlikely but wanted to go further than simply allowing Dyer to join the army's unemployed list. The first meeting of Montagu's Disorders committee was held on 21 April 1920, with a view to considering Dyer's actions in Amritsar on 13 April the previous year. The committee agreed that pursuing a conviction against Dyer was futile but that they should condemn his actions.

As tardy as ever, the government of India finally published its response to the Hunter Report two months after its release on 3 May. The government said that it accepted that the civilian authorities were wrong to hand over to the military without also advising and guiding it on any action that should be taken. It also criticised Dyer for not making the Proclamation more widely known, for not first warning the crowd before giving the order to fire, for allowing firing to continue for the length of time it did and for not helping the dead and the wounded. However, the government deftly passed the matter of how best to deal with Dyer on to the commander in chief, who it thought should be the one to take 'appropriate' action, without attempting to define what that action might be. It had successfully sidestepped its responsibility via a telegraph to England on the very day Dyer and his wife reached England.

When Reginald Dyer stepped off the hospital boat that had brought him home, a *Daily Mail* reporter and photographer were keenly waiting. Their resourcefulness afforded them great material as a defiant Dyer defended himself in an angry tirade in which he explained it was his duty to shoot in order to preserve the Raj, that he had been supported by superior officers, that he had not been court martialled and had never been given the opportunity to defend himself. He was right on the last three points at least. His comments made headlines that were to cause questions in the House and send Montagu into a frenzy of activity. He quickly circulated a draft of his Disorders Committee's latest conclusions from a meeting held on 5 May.

The Committee had drafted the Government's response to the Hunter Report and the government of India's Resolution, and discussed Dyer's interview with the press. The Committee's findings made it clear that the Government stood for no more force and/or loss of life than is necessary in conflict, and that Dyer's actions violated this intention. It also condemned the fact that Dyer gave no warning to the crowd at Amritsar and said that he was wrong to not offer medical assistance. The Committee also stated that Dyer did not have the right to punish an unarmed crowd who were unaware of his Proclamation. It called for the commander in chief to direct Dyer to retire. Montagu's aim to get the matter dealt with swiftly led him to ask if the Committee's conclusions could be brought before the Cabinet, at the same time distributing a copy of the Hunter Report to its members.

A copy of the Disorders Committee's conclusions also arrived in the War Office – the department responsible for the administration of the British army (now known as the Ministry of Defence). And it was to cause problems for Montagu and Churchill from then on in. The War Office immediately noticed the last recommendation of the findings – that the commander in chief should force Dyer's retirement. This was a snub to the War Office, which was up in arms, as this move fell within the remit of the Army Council, the supreme administrative body of the British army. Churchill was therefore obliged to write on behalf of his department to point out that the government of India, the Commander in Chief of India, the British government and the Secretary of State for India were not in a position to call for an officer's retirement. And that nothing should be published until the correct procedure had been followed.

Meanwhile, Dyer, now settled in lodgings just off Piccadilly, had begun to find a league of supporters – typically Conservative politicians and those opposed to reforms in India. When he learnt that his case was to come before the Army Council, he asked to be there, to be able to present his argument. Montagu, meanwhile, had shown the Disorders Committee's conclusions to the Cabinet and they had largely accepted its recommendations. The tussle between Montagu, Churchill, the Army Council and the Military Members of the Army Council began. The Army Council for its part did not want to be told what to do by civil servants, or to be bypassed by politicians. The Military Members did not want to see a brother in arms offered as a sacrifice to appease Indian reformists. Montagu wanted the process dealt with speedily, while Churchill did not want another minister running his show. In the end, the Army Council met on 14 May to examine Dyer's case. They had the report submitted by Dyer on 25 August to work from rather than the Hunter Report. The Army Council chose to defer any decisions until word came from the Commander in Chief of India, Monro.

Montagu published the official view; that Dyer had used excessive force, causing unnecessary loss of life and suffering and that the resignation of Dyer was supported, acknowledging that the case was now to come before the Army Council. The press, notably the *Morning Post*, began to rally around Dyer. The retired Roman Catholic Archbishop of Simla also supported the man now cast as the Saviour of the Punjab and many letters of support were printed in *The Times*, the *Post* and the other major newspapers. It's reasonable to believe that, while Dyer knew he would not get his command back, he felt he could still salvage some of his reputation and have the chance to defend himself publicly. His supporters were typically those that politically opposed Montagu and their motives may have been more self-serving than simply born out of concern for a wronged soldier.

The Army Council met again on 9 June, having refused to hear Dyer in person but said that it would accept a written statement. It would be composed with the help of a solicitor and a barrister – and would be a political document, designed for maximum effect. The day after the Army Council met, the press published scathing comments about Montagu given by O'Dwyer, who maintained Dyer's image of hero of India. O'Dwyer claimed Montagu misled the House over the chronology of his learning about events at the Jallianwala Bagh. O'Dwyer also demanded to see the War Office and the Prime Minister over the matter but was refused an audience with both. The Military Members of the Army Council also attempted to stir up trouble suggesting constitutional irregularities. All this discord was used as a stick to beat Montagu with by those opposed to reform in India. More and more, the events in Amritsar became less about the shooting and more about what could be made from it.

On 3 July, Dyer's legal team submitted its twenty-three-page report, including the proof of the support he'd received from his superior officers. Within the report, he complained about being punished without a trial. He explained that he had offered no warning that his men were about to fire because hesitation would have been dangerous and that as groups of men were forming potentially to surge forward, he had to direct fire at them until the crowd dispersed. He claimed his action had brought calm to the region and throughout the report used the term 'insurrection' to explain his motives behind the shooting, as within the official 'Manual of Military Law' insurrection allowed any degree of force to be used. He suggested that the crowd was part of an organised rebellion, not innocent bystanders. He left the wounded because they were not ordinary citizens but rebels and he trivialised the Crawling Order. The report concluded with his service record and referenced the Resolution the Government of India published in April 1919, in which it had promised to support officers involved in the uprising.

Dyer's statement was forwarded to the Chief of the Imperial General Staff, Sir Henry Wilson, whose role it was to coordinate army administration. In turn, Wilson delegated the job of dealing with it to General Sir Charles Harington Harington, who summarised the Council's point of view using Dyer's report almost entirely and rejecting the British government's position. When the Army Council published its assessment, it said it supported the view that Dyer had simply made an error of judgement, and it accepted the decisions made by the Indian Army. Since the Commander in Chief of India had removed Dyer from his post, passed him over for promotion or further employment and he was now on half pay, the Council reported that it felt no further action was necessary.

When Churchill received this statement, he refused to accept it and asked the Army Council to change its views in line with that of the Cabinet. But the Military Members on the Army Council refused and Churchill failed to convince them Dyer's retirement was necessary. In fact, all that had been achieved by consulting the Army Council was a one-month delay in the process of dealing with Dyer. This wasted time and the failure of Churchill to make the Army Council agree with ministers became ammunition for those determined to fight on Dyer's behalf. And it was an embarrassing defeat for both Churchill and Montagu.

The day after the Army Council published its conclusions, the next full Cabinet meeting was due. Churchill was forced to present the Army Council's views to the Cabinet, which concluded compulsory retirement was not necessary for Dyer and that Churchill must now communicate the Army Council's decision to the House that afternoon. While the announcement was the end of Dyer's hopes for a trial and reinstatement, it was the beginning of much deliberation within parliament. And a Commons debate on Dyer was scheduled for the 8th – a debate that was to prove disastrous for the career of Montagu and become a shining example of how Dyer's actions came to have endless political ramifications.

The debate over Dyer's future held much political significance for the Liberal Unionist coalition government led by Lloyd George, which was keen to push through the Montagu-Chelmsford Reforms. While the coalition had a massive majority – with over five times as many seats in the House – the views of the (Conservative) Unionists often clashed with the Liberals. Many MPs were of course ex-services and not keen on reforms in India – and particularly not those dreamt up by a Liberal

Jew. These MPs were also often well connected to the upper echelons of British India, to whom reform only meant loss of status and income. The maintenance of the Empire was a major issue at the time, dividing the coalition and Dyer and his actions therefore brought to the surface far wider issues. The press was also highly critical of the Liberal party and keen to highlight any controversy that occurred.

The Commons debate was scheduled for 4pm on 8 July and ran on into the evening, lasting more than five hours. Montagu, Churchill and the Leader of the Commons (and future Prime Minister) Andrew Bonar Law planned to put forward the government view. Wracked with anxiety in the lead up to the debate however, Montagu ended up delivering an emotional tirade rather than a factual, planned speech from notes. It was met with uproar and those who did not agree with him were quick to mock and bait him. Critics heckled Montagu with claims that if the government didn't support Dyer in this instance, every soldier would lose faith in what was his duty. There were claims from Sir William Johnson-Hicks that a massive majority of Indian Civil servants and British in India supported Dyer and that there was a real rebellion akin to the Mutiny afoot – Dyer had saved the day. Others fretted about British prestige and quoted patriotic letters in support of Dyer.

Churchill gave a skilful presentation however, calling Dyer's actions monstrous and that his censure was a moral necessity. He argued – with some support – that Dyer had abandoned the British military principle of minimum force. It was suggested Dyer's behaviour tarnished the reputation of the British. But Mr Palmer and Conservative MP Rupert Gwynne attacked Churchill, referring to his decisions in Gallipoli and Antwerp, saying that Dyer's error was slight compared to the lives lost then. Palmer went on to attack Montagu's speech and demand an inquiry into the treatment of Dyer. Gwynne also attacked the Secretary of State for India, accusing him of misleading the House over the events, saying he should have told Ministers about Amritsar sooner. Montagu was so angered by this, when he stood to disagree he became totally incoherent.

Finally, Bonar Law spoke to sum up. He tried to calm the House, picking out the facts from the fury. He reminded everyone that the Government dispatch censuring Dyer was not just the work of Montagu but represented the views of the entire Cabinet. He said that Dyer had found himself in a difficult position and had indeed made a proclamation that was defied; he was in danger in the Bagh as his troops were few. But, he added, the Hunter Committee was right to find two faults with the actions Dyer took – namely, the fact he gave no warning to the crowd and that he continued to have his men fire for a significant length of time. Law said that Dyer had made a grave mistake and that the government must reject the idea that punishment may be dealt out for an effect upon others. He said the Army Council had acted correctly, that Dyer had no right to a Court Martial and that no action should be taken against Dyer. Finally, he explained that all the military people he had discussed the issue with agreed Dyer was in the wrong – and the government cannot support its servants when their actions are wrong.

The divided House voted and the government won by 101 votes. But of the 129 against, 119 were Unionists from the Coalition ranks. The debate was over but while it signalled the end of any hope for Dyer that he might be reinstated and exonerated it was just the start of more problems for Montagu, who left the proceedings to calls for his resignation. After the debate, Montagu was said to be depressed and he wrote to the government of India apologising for the way in which the whole process had been handled. Chelmsford showed little sympathy for the man he'd never really liked, and the Viceroy's Private Secretary, J.L. Maffey, was also contemptuous. The War Office wrote officially to Dyer, to tell him what had been decided. He resigned on 17 July, but it was not the end of his infamy.

On the day of the Commons debate, the *Morning Post* set up an appeal to raise funds for Dyer's defense case. It raised close to £600 in the first twelve hours and started an avalanche of letters of support and gifts for the Dyers. The *Post* continued the momentum by then analysing the debate in its pages on the 9th, contrasting the deaths caused by Dyer in the Jallianwala Bagh (379 officially) and those 'caused' by Churchill in the Battle of Antwerp (300 deaths and 2,000 British captives) and Gallipoli (41,211 killed and captured). A similar appeal by the *Pioneer* paper in India was also underway and by August fundraising there had raised a total of £7,480 15s. In India, the government tried to ban the collections for Dyer as it was against military rules but it was widely ignored.

Ironically, as the British in India were digging deep for Dyer, the government there was still dragging its heels over compensation payouts to those widowed and orphaned by the massacre. These payments were in stark contrast to those paid to British dependants of those murdered during the disturbances – who received a total of 400,321 rupees compared to a total of 13,840 rupees received by those dependants of Indians killed in the Jallianwala Bagh. Mrs Stewart – the wife of the murdered bank manager in Amritsar city – was awarded 20,000 rupees, while a compensation fee of 500 rupees was allowed for each of the dead of the massacre. The Punjab government was also increasing taxes to cover the money spent during the imposition of martial law in areas that saw uprisings.

The issue also attracted so much attention that it was inevitable that it would need to be considered in the House of Lords as well, where typically there was more Conservative support. A debate in the Lords was scheduled for 19 July, although ahead of that, the ex-Governor of Bombay Lord Sydenham asked the upper house if the India Office had applied pressure to the government of India to change its resolution for the 3 May dispatch. Sydenham was of course in cahoots with O'Dwyer, and the question certainly put the cat among the pigeons with Chelmsford denying the accusation by telegram.

When the day came, the first to rise was Viscount Finlay, who asked the Lords to move that Dyer had been treated unjustly and the process had set a dangerous precedent for every soldier facing rebellion in the future. He claimed that the length of firing at Amritsar was justified because of the effect it would have and that it was not using terror (or 'frightfulness' as it was called) as a method. He also criticised Montagu for the stigma he had placed on Dyer. In reply, Lord Sinha spoke for the Government; he denied the government of India had changed its story or orchestrated a cover up. He argued Dyer's own words had condemned him and that the decision to fire in Amritsar to teach a lesson across the Punjab was wrong.

The debate carried on until 11pm – breaking for dinner – and started again the next day. The arguments against Dyer included the fact that the assembled crowd was not a legitimate target, that his troops were not in any danger in Jallianwala Bagh, that the principle of firing on some to frighten others was fundamentally wrong and that his actions were incomparable to anything that had gone before in colonial history. Rather than save the Punjab, it was argued, Dyer had created bitterness against the British in India. Lord Birkenhead warned that if the Lords agreed with the motion, it would effectively mean that they were going against the Hunter Committee, the government of India, the Commander in Chief of India, the Cabinet and the Army Council.

But many chose to stand behind Dyer and his actions, certain that he was facing a rebellion similar to the Mutiny and not just an isolated riot. Dyer was portrayed as a gallant soldier with his recent campaign in Thal mentioned. Instead, it was the government of India that was in the wrong by not holding its own inquiry and instead passing the buck to the Hunter Committee. It was also wrong in that Dyer was never given a fair trial but was judged instead by the Hunter Committee. Those who agreed with the motion wanted the broader implications considered; if the government would not support Dyer here, in what position did it leave other officers in similar circumstances? Order must be maintained – and all punishment acted as a deterrent, contended the Marquess of Salisbury.

The government was humiliated; when the votes were cast there were 129 votes in favour of the motion and just 86 against it. Of course, the Lords were typically also members of the aristocracy and therefore invested in the continuation of the Empire just as it was. While Dyer and his supporters may have felt triumphant, votes in the upper or lower houses made no difference to actual government policy. The fallout was perhaps more subtle however as the defeat of Montagu and the Coalition's Liberal principles here had longer-lasting implications at home and back in India. On a personal level for Montagu, after the debates, ninety-three MPs signed a petition calling for his resignation. The Secretary of State for India ignored the calls to quit, but his popularity was in a downwards spiral and he was later forced to resign and then lost his seat in the next general election. He died in 1924, aged just forty-five. It's possible this lack of political support worked against the reforms he had put in place in India. The Conservative party was able to use the criticism leveled at the Liberal party for its own end, increasing its majority and winning the 1922 general election. The Conservative party was less keen on reform and Indian independence of any sort, as it comprised those who had the most to lose if the 'Jewel in the Crown' became less profitable for its owner. Could it be that it is this political divide that still prevents British politicians from coming together to properly condemn the events even today?

The apparent indifference displayed by the Commons and the Lords over the suffering caused by Dyer worked to alienate the people of India. The Government in Simla also never publicly dealt with those criticised in the Hunter Report and for the natives, that meant no one had been punished. In the military, nothing was done in response to the findings, Dyer lost his job but was never formally accused of any crime, other officers involved simply faded away and in one case even received a promotion. The government of India did write to the Punjab administration criticising Kitchin and Irving, listing their mistakes, and pointing out that they should have remained involved in decision-making. After this, Kitchin resigned but Irving stayed on and – perhaps shockingly – later received a knighthood. But the government of India was still slow to act on the matter, adding insult to injury, proving that considering the feelings of the Indian population was not a top priority.

British India was delighted with the result of the debate in the House of Lords and wasted no time in revelling in it, as did the British press in the colony. This worked to further damage the relationship between the two races and those Indians that had admired the British principles of justice and morality felt betrayed, instead believing that their rulers held them in low regard. This feeling was particularly poignant in the Indian political classes, many of whom were lawyers and had been brought up to admire the British education system and lifestyle, seeking to be part of it. The lack of compassion from both the British establishment and the government of India worked to alienate many of those who had been committed to dominion-style self-government for an India that remained within the Empire. This was true of Gandhi and other Indian leaders and it was to be another of the far-reaching effects that became the legacy of the Amritsar Massacre.

On 14 February 1920, an appeal started for a Jallianwala Bagh Memorial Fund. A committee had bought the Bagh for 540,000 rupees so that it could become a permanent symbol of what had happened there and a focus for the nationalist movement that grew from the fallout of the events. The initial purchasers were Gandhi, Madan Mohan Malaviya, Motilal Nehru, Swami Shraddhanand, Harkishan Lal, Kitchlew and Girdhari Lal. The *Bombay Chronicle* boosted the appeal by covering the campaign – and it continued to snowball.

On 30 May, the All India Congress Committee met and passed two resolutions. The first requested that the British Parliament take General

Dyer, Colonel Johnson, Colonel O'Brien and Mr. Bosworth-Smith to trial to answer for their crimes. The second resolution was an attack on the racism within the majority Hunter Report, which by overlooking the inhumane acts carried out at Amritsar and failing to take to task the governments of India and the Punjab for those acts, had proved how little regard the British had for Indians. Respected Indians who had worked within and alongside the establishment began to turn their back on British India. Motilal Nehru withdrew from constitutional politics and began to support Gandhi. Resigning from the United Provinces Council, he abandoned his practice at the Bar and burned all his foreign clothes and belongings. Instead he wore a khadi, made of the homespun cloth typically used by the poor of India, in a move to support native industries.

In August, Gandhi wrote to the Viceroy voicing his concerns about the British and Indian governments. He argued that the measures taken by Dyer were out of proportion to the offences which any Indians may have committed. He complained about Chelmsford's lenient treatment of Dyer, his ignorance about events in the Punjab, the exoneration of Dyer and the disregard for the resentment the House of Lords caused by supporting the General. He added that he had misgivings about the future of the Empire and could no longer be loyal to it.

Dyer's actions alone may not have irrevocably damaged the relationship between the British Raj and her subjects, but the British reaction to the Hunter Report (or rather the lack thereof) and the government of India's insensitivity after the disturbances were certainly major factors in its breakdown. The lack of public punishment for Dyer and the cavalier attitude to the suffering of the people of the Punjab, meant that the educated classes of India became disillusioned with the Empire they had admired, and cost the Raj the respect of its citizens across the entire social spectrum of India.

Chapter 9

A Controversy that Wouldn't End

After the debates in parliament, Dyer's health was worse than it had ever been and he went to seek medical advice in Harrogate. There he was diagnosed with arteriosclerosis, a serious condition where arteries become clogged with fatty substances called plaques, or atheroma. These plaques cause the arteries to harden and narrow, restricting the blood flow and oxygen supply to vital organs, and increasing the risk of blood clots, heart attacks and strokes. At that time, treatment options were limited but rest and avoiding excitement was recommended. To this end, Dyer and Annie went to stay with a friend in Dumfries.

However, Dyer struggled to find the peace and quiet he and his wife may have sought with both well-meaning supporters and those with their own political and professional motives for continuing to keep his actions at Amritsar in the spotlight. To begin with, the *Post* continued with its fundraising appeal, collecting both in England and via its Calcutta correspondent. Editor H.A. Gwynne closed the fund on 6 December 1920, by which time the total had reached £26,317 1s 10d, with the eventual amount received coming to about £28,000, comparable to £813,615 today using the national archives currency converter. The donations came from all around the world in varying forms from cash and cheques to jewellery, stamps and valuable books. £9,360 came from India. Along with the donations were letters of support. The owner of the *Post* wanted to present the money to Dyer in a political show, doubtless thinking of his own headlines. But Dyer turned down the opportunity, perhaps because he was not well enough to travel and be in the public eye, instead opting to send a written thank you. The paper did however run a story titled 'A Debt Acknowledged' in which it claimed that the fund went some way to remove the stigma of national ingratitude. Dyer's letter, in which he thanked people for their support and sympathy, was quoted. He also used the correspondence to emphasize that he was saving 'women and children and life generally' by his actions – and explained that he hoped the generous donations would be seen as a reflection of the 'general trend of public feeling in this matter'.

Sir Michael O'Dwyer was also unable to let go of the criticism of Dyer – and by association – himself. He started a two-year campaign of letter writing, harassing every official in India and England in an attempt to clear the names of those censured in the Hunter Report. He was never successful, but doubtless he continued to be a nuisance and prevented Dyer's name being quietly forgotten.

After Dumfries, Annie and Dyer moved down to Wiltshire where they had bought their son Geoff a farm. Geoff was to build a successful dairy business and the Dyers lived there for about five years. Having partly recovered, Dyer embarked upon a political career, writing an article for the right-wing paper the *Globe* in 1921. The piece was part of a series entitled 'The Peril to the Empire' and previous contributors had included Lord Sydenham and O'Dwyer. Dyer's submission, 'India's Path to Suicide', expressed his belief that self-rule was a ridiculous concept. Within the article, he painted a romanticised and out-of-date view of the Raj, portraying the natives as simple, looking to their sahib for protection and guidance. He surmised that, left to their own devices, the natives would simply argue among themselves. He also managed to mention that the Punjab disturbances were part of an organised rebellion and he had saved the day.

Perhaps buoyed by this small stage, Dyer decided that he wanted to officially be able to use the title General, a rank he had filled temporarily and had forfeited when he gave up command of 5 Brigade. His timing was not the best, as the India Office was about to be granted delegated powers to handle such honours, and Edwin Montagu was still in place. The British administration Dyer was familiar with had also changed. There was a move to reconciliation, and with the Montagu-Chelmsford reforms in place, the Legislative Assembly had been created. There was even a new Viceroy – Lord Reading – who was of an entirely different persuasion to Winchester- and Oxford-educated Chelmsford. Lord Reading had made his very first official visit to the city of Amritsar, visited the Jallianwala Bagh and ordered an increase in compensation to the victims of the massacre. In this world Dyer was a dinosaur.

So Dyer was forced, on 9 February, to make his application for the retention of the honorary title of Brigadier to the Under-Secretary of State at the India Office. Here was a bureaucratic hot potato – which the India Office recognised – and passed back to the War Office, using the date of application as the reason it was not their responsibility. The War Office in turn passed it along to the Military Members of the Army Council for a decision which, not surprisingly, was that they saw no reason to withhold the title (it was standard practice to award the title if personnel had spent six months service in a higher rank). The Council then instructed the India Office to publish the news in the *London Gazette*, but it refused, asking instead that the Council do it. The to-ing and fro-ing meant that the deadline for publication passed and the opportunity to award the title was missed.

At the time, Dyer's personal plans were focussed on writing and publishing a book about his campaign in East Persia. *The Raiders of the Sarhadd* allowed Dyer to cast himself as a brave soldier and hero of the Punjab. Doubtless this is how he wanted his military career to be remembered – and as a General – but since the controversy over the Massacre at Amritsar has never died down, his book is little known, whereas the actions at the Jallianwala Bagh and thereafter are infamous in the history of the Empire, and its decline. However, the book did prove to be a massive ego boost at the time as Dyer also embarked on a series of lectures to promote the title. During this time, Dyer drew much support from his audience and at one of his talks he was presented with an obsequious memorial book created by a committee of British ladies in India. Filled with signatures, it included a highly complimentary dedication to him, and despaired that their hero had been poorly treated. The ladies also sent a gold watch.

The application for the award of Dyer's honorary rank was still a bone of contention. The Army Council was not happy that the issue remained unresolved and wrote to the India Office about the matter. This was a military matter and not political, the Council argued. But Montagu and the new Viceroy pushed back that, despite the threat from the Council, it would appeal to the Cabinet if necessary. The new Secretary of State for War waded in, supporting the Council and writing to Montagu, and then Churchill. Finally, General Sir Claude Jacob, the Chief of the General Staff in India became involved – and he had the trump card. Sir Claude went to the War Office himself and explained that the timing was wrong; to make this award now could bring unrest just as the Prince of Wales was due to tour India. And nothing trumps a member of the Royal Family visiting its Empire. The matter was dropped.

In November 1924, O'Dwyer continued his campaign against the criticism of the military action taken in the Punjab and in this instance, a personal slight in the book *Gandhi and Anarchy*, written by Sir C. Sankaran Nair. Nair was a moderate Indian politician and a former lawyer, who in 1904 was appointed Companion of the Indian Empire by the King-Emperor. An early President of the Indian National Congress, Nair favoured reforms and self-government and opposed Gandhi. He was a member of the Viceroy's Executive Council in 1915 in charge of Education but resigned in protest over the Indian administration in 1919. Although Nair's book targeted Gandhi, it blamed O'Dwyer for the atrocities in the Punjab, on the basis he gave Dyer his consent and blessing. O'Dwyer sued, demanding a retraction, an apology and a charitable donation.

The large court case collected together many witnesses, arguably all of those involved in Amritsar bar one, Dyer, thought to be on his deathbed. Dyer's poor physical health played a starring role in the five-week long trial, with O'Dwyer using it to get 'a final hearing from a living jury' for his reportedly dying friend. The judge certainly felt sympathy for the military officers and directed the jury as such, with the resulting decisions favouring O'Dwyer eleven to one. He was awarded £500 damages and costs. Dyer's still loyal army of supporters claimed this case as his vindication. In India, Europeans hailed the victory. Dyer was also told of the outcome of the case.

The case led to more questions in the Houses, although the format was now different, with Ramsay MacDonald's Labour government in power since the 1924 election. In the Lords, Lord Olivier, new at the India Office, blamed the Lords' 1920 resolution for the political problems India now faced, while a Conservative MP in the Commons asked for debate to consider revoking Dyer's censure. There were also calls for Judge McCardie, who presided over the O'Dwyer case, to be removed from the bench. Ramsay MacDonald came down firmly on the new furore, announcing that the government completely accepted the decision of the government of the day. And that was the end of parliament's interest in Dyer. Armed with this stand, Lord Olivier sent a dispatch to the Indian government relating that the government adheres to the principal of using minimal force and that it is not acceptable for one officer to punish people for an effect elsewhere. The government of India repeated these values in a Proclamation of its own.

Dyer died in July 1927, following a second stroke caused by his arteriosclerosis. But even in death, he was still being used as a political puppet. His funeral on the 28th was a grand affair – unusually so for an officer of his rank. His body lay in rest for the morning at the Guard's Chapel, in the Wellington Barracks, on the south side of St. James's Park in London, the only Royal Military Chapel in the city. At 1.30pm, the coffin left the Barracks to process along Horse Guards Parade off Whitehall, on its way to St Martin-in-the-Fields at the northeast corner of Trafalgar Square. The cortège consisted of four horses, mounted soldiers, a gun carriage, guardsmen and family and civilian mourners on foot, followed by three cars and fifty more marching soldiers. Dyer's coffin was draped in the Union Jack and piled high with his medals and swords, and there were large wreaths and flowers sent from all over the world. Roads were closed and the press was in attendance.

More mourners waited at St Martin's including Major General Beynon and Brigadier General Moberley and many of the men that had served under Dyer who remained resolutely loyal to him. The military was keen to be seen to be supporting their former colleague, happily praising Dyer as a brave soldier to the reporters. Members of the Imperial establishment also attended, including the Secretary to the Governor of India, who was also a member of the Viceroy's Council and a representative on behalf of the Home Secretary. By now, Stanley Baldwin's Conservative government was in power, and this funeral was quite a show of British traditionalists. Rudyard Kipling, who was born in India and was very much in favour of imperialism, believing in an innate British superiority over the natives, also sent a large wreath. At the end of the church service, a bugler sounded the Last Post, and the coffin continued on its journey to Golders Green Crematorium in North West London. According to his wishes, the floral tributes received for Dyer were placed at official national war memorial, the Cenotaph.

Dyer's death gave his supporters a further opportunity to relive his story of heroism – especially to the press – as the funeral was covered both at home and in India. Invariably, the papers printed the story with the angle that best suited the political persuasions of their audience, with readers also submitting letters of support for their chosen cause. The event was quite the spectacle, not least because the locations and permissions required to host and support it demonstrated that this officer represented much more than a long-serving soldier would normally.

The funeral was more in tune with the type of honour usually reserved for a national hero, and it's unclear who decided that the inconvenience of road closures and the like was justified, and who paid the cost of adequate policing and security.

While Annie Dyer chose not to publish the last resting place of her husband's ashes and did not have a memorial stone made, O'Dwyer was determined to have a lasting memory to honour his officer. He formed the Dyer Memorial Committee to raise funds for a permanent memorial, eventually opting to use the money to endow a bed or wing within a private hospital in Simla that was open to the wives and families of army officers. The telegram approaching the hospital however ended up with the new Viceroy Lord Irwin, who was well aware that the hospital now served many Indian officers and that any reference to Dyer would be more than awkward. Irwin contacted the Secretary of State in London, Lord Birkenhead for guidance, who replied advising that the offer was declined. In early 1928, the hospital wrote to the Memorial Committee, suggesting the offer would be a better fit with an British institution. Instead Annie decided not to pursue the idea further.

In 1923, a Trust organised by Gandhi and Congress bought the Jallianwala Bagh to place a memorial on the site, paid for with donations from the public. Designed by American architect Benjamin Kauffman Polk and Indian architect Suraj P. Subherwal, the memorial was constructed after independence in 1951 and inaugurated by the first President of India, Dr Rajendra Pasad, in 1961. The bullet holes in the wall, and the original well, where many died as they sought refuge from the hail of bullets, are preserved alongside the tall memorial building, a museum and an eternal flame. Recently a statue of Udham Singh was unveiled. A plaque at the memorial reads 'This place is saturated with the blood of about two thousand Hindus, Sikhs and Muslims who were martyred in a non-violent struggle', a number that Prince Phillip tactlessly suggested was 'a bit exaggerated' when he visited.

Chapter 10

The Rise of Indian Nationalism

The East India Trading Company, and the unreasonable demands placed upon Indians by it, is in a way responsible for the rise of organised Indian nationalism against British rule. While the Mutiny of 1857 was a reaction to the insensitive and corrupt administration by the Company and not a nationalist revolt, it was responsible for the very conception of the British Raj that the proponents of Indian nationalism would eventually unite to conquer. The deep divides caused by the Mutiny were never truly bridged, merely patched over with an underlying mistrust on both sides remaining, a mistrust that would colour all future motivations and behaviour. A mistrust that would leave Reginald Dyer in a position where raining bullets onto a crowd of unarmed civilians seemed an acceptable way to deal with perceived political dissenters.

In truth, India had been colonized by various rulers, including Ashoka in the third century BC and the Mughals, a dynasty of Muslim emperors that moved into the area in the sixteenth century, prior to the British Empire. But the Indian nationalism that opposed the Raj did not follow a linear development, as the vastness of the continent and divergent races, cultures, religions, languages and social groups it spanned gave birth to both moderate and extremist views and many in between. Regional power struggles, influences and politics also meant that nationalism, far from being one voice, was a choir with not everyone singing from the same hymn sheet. Neither was it static with clear ideology and goals carved in stone, rather it evolved over time, steered in many directions by external events and the philosophies and self-interests of those at its helm. But it is clear that the success of the call for independence from the British was to become an unparalleled achievement.

During the years that the East India Company traded, Bombay, Calcutta and Madras had become prosperous and busy cities. This had led to the emergence of a group of native merchants who became wealthy traders and often invested in land, banking or other commercial ventures. These were the elite who began to also take up administrative and advisory roles in society, and they often formed groups that ensured their interests – both selfish and those with a wider sense of responsibility – were protected. Often, these groups would mediate between the British and the native masses. This was also the section of society that benefitted from the Western education that had begun to be available at the time, as working alongside the British was the best way to ensure a lucrative career. By providing university educations, the British had ensured there was a suitable pool of workers for their judicial and administrative systems. However, this group of educated Indians was also exposed to Western politics and philosophies and gradually wanted a say in how government was run. It would be these people who went on to question government policies and lead the nationalist movement first against the Company and then the Raj.

One of the first moves of the educated Indian elite was to establish the British Indian Association on 31 October 1851. Most of the early leaders of the British Indian Association were Conservatives by tradition and temperament, although some were more progressive. The group was an amalgamation of the Landholders' Society and the Bengal British India Society, which hoped to secure the welfare and interests of Indians across the board. The British Indian Association petitioned the government and British parliament on various grievances. The Association had similar groups across the country, and while in isolation its achievements were few, it served to create a political consciousness in India and allowed more effective organisations – such as the Indian National Congress formed in 1885 – to follow in its footsteps. The educated classes took up roles that allowed them to travel, helping them to spread their ideas and come into contact with others of similar leanings. Many of them were involved in the press, at the very least contributing to it. Eventually, the Native Press Association was formed, a group designed to serve the interest of a free press.

It was at this time that the idea that the lucrative British Raj was making Indians poorer rather than better off began to surface. It touched on the issue of an increasing tax burden the people had to pay to support the system and discussed the exploitation of India's resources via exportation. This came to be known as the 'drain theory' and would be wholeheartedly supported by many nationalists in the future including Gandhi, and most recently Shashi Tharoor.

But not all nationalists, or those with nationalist sympathies, were Indian. George Frederick Samuel Robinson, 1st Marquess of Ripon, who took the Viceroyalty in 1880 under the Gladstone administration, repealed the Vernacular Press Act, enacted in 1878 by his predecessor Lord Lytton, which was designed to curtail the freedom of the Indian-language press. Lord Ripon was a committed Liberal and served in every Liberal cabinet from 1861 until the year before his death in 1909. In India, he encouraged the spread of education, supported local self-government and promoted political activity. Ripon also became known for his work on the Ilbert Bill of 1883, through which he tried to make good racial discrimination in the rural law courts that forbade legally qualified Indians to try white defendants. British India – and even those in London – was furious, believing that an Indian should never judge his natural superior, a white European. Detractors went as far as to fundraise and form the Defence Association to fight the changes. Ripon had to back down, and a diluted version of the bill went through instead. The disappointment kindled nationalist feelings and was instrumental in the formation of the Indian National Congress, which met in Bombay in 1885.

Political reformer Allan Octavian Hume, who worked in the Indian Civil Service, first conceived of the British Committee Indian National Congress. It aimed to bring together the various educated groups and their developing sense of national identity and unity and provide them with a political voice. It raised issues brought by Indian barrister W.C. Bonnerjee, who was the first president of the Indian National Congress, and Parsi Dadabhoi Naoroji, who was to become a Liberal Party MP in 1882, to the attention of British parliament. The first Chair of this British Congress group was William Wedderburn, a Scottish politician who had worked as a civil servant in India. At first it was far from reactionary and could have been seen as a way for the British Raj to gauge native opinion. Originally, Congress was designed to meet once a year, each time in a different place, to discuss pertinent issues and form resolutions. The issues discussed ranged from how the Civil Service could be improved to increasing native participation in Council administration. Success for the legislative reforms the Congress called for came in 1892 when the British parliament passed the Indian Councils Act.

In 1905, however, the placid nature of Congress began to change with a second generation of those involved in Congress coming to the fore. At this time, Lord Curzon, a British Conservative, was Viceroy, a position he had held since 1899. A dedicated head of administration in many ways, he had worked to restore Indian monuments such as the Taj Mahal, but made the mistake of partitioning Bengal, which resulted in the separation of the largely Muslim eastern areas from the largely Hindu western areas. Bengal was also home for much of Indian's westernised elite and cynics suggested that it was no accident that this change in borders had happened to the politically outspoken section of society. The Hindus of West Bengal complained that the division would make them a minority in their own province. The resulting backlash spread quickly to other places such as Bombay and protestors boycotted British-made goods and called for a tax revolt, political actions that led to demands for self-government. The Bombay partition effectively pitted the educated Hindus – who had previously held the British in high regard – against the Raj. The move to partition ended Curzon's career and by stirring up nationalist feeling across the classes, went on to have far reaching results.

As with most political groups, there were some schisms within Congress, with some sections of society feeling less represented. One group that seemed to stand apart from the educated Hindu elite entrenched in India's political life was the Muslim population. In response to this, in 1906 the All-India Muslim League was formed. The group grew out of a literary movement founded by the reformist and philosopher Syed Ahmad Khandf but developed to define and advance the civil rights of India's elite Muslims. A two-nation state – in which Muslims would gain their own land – was always part of the League's philosophy. The League often disagreed with the aims and work of Congress, and at various times worked to support the Raj. The League was also responsible for Muslims being identified as a separate community to the Hindus. Only later would the League work to serve the interests of Muslims at all socio-economic levels. The main difference between Congress and the League however was that the League sought mainly to ensure that the rights of Muslims were protected under whatever system prevailed, while Congress had a wider political focus which extended to looking towards future self-rule.

Central Punjab was richly irrigated agricultural land, and strategically important to the British Raj because the majority of the Indian army was typically recruited there. In 1906, a new Punjab Land Colonisation bill was implemented in the province but was poorly-received, with detractors fearing the increased rates of land revenue and irrigation tax was an attack on landholding rights. The first of the protests was organised in the Chenab Colony, an area that was most affected by the British move to stop further land fragmentation via the practice of primogeniture - passing land down from father to son. The farmers there regarded this action as an unjustified interference with their traditional rights covering the division of property. Further agitations spread throughout the Punjab with riots in Lahore, Lyallpur and Rawalpindi, with the reformist Hindu group Arya Samaj joining the fight. Nationalist leaders Lala Lajpat Rai and Ajit Singh emerged but rather than negotiate, the British government response was to deport Lala and Singh to Burma and prosecute a newspaper for sedition.

Over the next few years, British India would see a series of attacks on the establishment. In December 1907, Hindu terrorists used a bomb to derail a train carrying the Viceroy's chief assistant and in April the following year, a bomb was thrown into a railway carriage with the intent of killing a white civil servant. The bomb instead killed two British ladies, a Mrs Kennedy and her daughter. It was masterminded by members of the Ghose family who lived in Alipore near Calcutta. This distinguished Bombay family had a bomb factory in their garden and Barindra Ghose, his brother Cambridge graduate Aurobindo and twenty-seven others were arrested for the crime, including leading politician B.G. Tilak. Nineteen of those arrested were convicted, three were hanged and Tilak was exiled. In retaliation, Ghose supporters tracked down the prosecutors, killing first a police inspector in 1908, then the public prosecutor the following year. Lieutenant Colonel Sir William Curzon Wyllie was also connected to the case and was assassinated at a reception at the Imperial Institute in July 1909. A doctor, Cowasji Lalkaka attempted to disarm the assassin but was also shot and died. The killer was the son of a doctor, and a student at University College, London. Punjabi Madan Lal Dhingra was a member of the Hindu Nationalist terror group Abhinav Bharat Sanstha, formed after Bengal partition by Vinayak Savarkar. Madan Lal Dhingra was quickly sentenced and found guilty. The actions of the group convinced Gandhi, who knew the founder Savarkar, that he must steer nationalists away from violence, instead finding an approach that Indians could be spiritually proud of.

The Indian Councils Act in 1909, more commonly known as the Morley-Minto Reforms, was the British Raj's first real concessions to Indian participation in government and helped to satisfy some nationalists for some time. Viceroy Minto, who was in favour of reform, handed over his role to Charles Hardinge, 1st Baron Hardinge of Penshurst, who was of a similar outlook. These reformist ideas led to the reversal of the controversial Bengal partition and the move of the Raj capital from Calcutta to Delhi, a choice popular with Indians. But in 1912, an attempt was made to assassinate Lord and Lady Hardinge in Delhi by a Hindu terrorist, and in May the following year a bomb killed a junior minister in Lahore. Many Indians were still not happy with the token gestures the Raj offered and wanted more effective changes. Bengal was also affected by increasing revolutionary violence; figures show that in 1914 there were fourteen terrorist attacks in the area, but that just a year later the figure had risen to thirty-six. Clearly there was increased pressure on the Raj.

By 1914, militant nationalist Tilak was also out of prison, and he and Annie Besant, a British socialist, activist and supporter of both Irish and Indian self-rule, created a series of Home Rule Leagues around the country. While Tilak's group concentrated its efforts mostly in western India, Besant set up at Madras and focused on a nationwide approach. The groups hoped to rally Indian public opinion for self-government and were designed to force the British to offer Indian independence in return for support for the war in Europe. The groups amassed over 60,000 full-time members, making them far more popular than Congress. Their appeal grew when Muslim nationalist lawyer Muhammad Ali Jinnah joined. Pressure from the movement contributed to the drafting of the Montagu Declaration in 1917 by Edwin Samuel Montagu, Secretary of State for India, which in turn laid the groundwork for political reforms in India instituted by Britain after the First World War. Jinnah and the Home Rule Leagues also impressed Congress, which signed the Lucknow Pact in December 1916 and agreed to the idea of separate electorates for Muslims and Hindus. The Pact paved the way for Hindu-Muslim cooperation, which was an important part of Gandhi's vision for an independent India.

Reform was also a response to more revolutionary activity however, with the Punjab being a hotspot for different groups hoping to use the First World War as an opportunity to flourish, while British attentions were elsewhere. Much of the trouble in the region was associated with the Sikh revolutionaries mentored in California in 1914 by Har Dayal and his group Ghadr, which was founded at Berkley University. The group grew strong in Canada and the USA where there were many Indian workers. Part of the group's aim was to encourage as many members as it could to return to India and stir up trouble, as well as to infiltrate the Indian Army to subvert the troops. At the start of the war, the German Embassy in Washington contacted Ghadr leaders offering funds and intelligence, hoping Ghadr's success would destabalise the Empire. In January 1915, the Ghadr group loaded 8,000 rifles and 4 million rounds of ammunition on a vessel bound for India from San Diego. The ship never made it and was instead forced into Washington, where the cargo was seized. Ghadr saw another failed plot in Canada when, again in cooperation with the German government, it tried to sabotage the railway in Vancouver.

Ghadr did however successfully engineer a mass transfer of supporters back to India, with German backing. The plan was to encourage Punjabi rebels to rise up, to infiltrate garrisons and cause disaffection among troops and to liberate Kashmir, Burma and Malay. The first ship arrived in Calcutta in 1915, filled with 400 Sikhs and 60 Muslims. The British however were waiting and managed to round up many as they got to shore; and the leaders were captured too as they had all arrived on one ship together. Despite this, between 1914 and 1917, it is estimated that around 8,000 Ghadr supporters returned to India, and mostly to the Punjab, although some did reach Calcutta, Madras and Columbo.

Ghadr successfully infiltrated many Indian army garrisons, including the Sikhs of 23rd Cavalry at Amritsar in 1914, which Gahdr planned to use in an attack on the magazine at Lahore. However, this resulted in arrest for the conspirators with twelve men from the 23rd Cavalry court martialled and executed. The revolutionary group continued its attempts to coordinate a rebellion among troops, but informers gave them away. Instead, regiments were searched and disarmed, with 180 Sikh soldiers in Lahore arrested, fourteen in Benares and five in Mandi. Ghadr leader N.J. Pingle was also caught after approaching the 12th cavalry and Meerut's 128th Pioneers and found to be in possession of explosives and subsequently hanged. Ghadr did have some success however; the 8th cavalry at Jhamsi murdered a commanding officer and wounded other officers before being overcome and Sikhs in 12th Pioneers in Arden and in Burma Military Police at Mandalay were affected. Some supporters also marched on the town of Jhar Sahib nearby and mounted a raid on the treasury at Ferozepore, although an approach to the 26th Punjabis stationed there was unsuccessful. Eventually, twenty-one Sikhs were convicted in the US of waging war against Britain, along with eighteen American and German nationals. More problems arose in Punjab when revolutionary Rash Behari Bose arrived on the scene. He was infamous for organising the attacks in Delhi in 1912 and 1913, and for the bomb attack on Lord Hardinge. He also worked with Ghadr which represented a problem for the British who had always used religious and class divisions in society to rule India. Joining with Ghadr proved to be worryingly effective. Bose's group was credited with forty-five serious attacks by February 1915, including an ambush on a railway bridge picquet at Amritsar where a guard was murdered and weapons taken. Bose set up his headquarters at Amritsar and then Lahore. Since much of the power of the British Raj was about keeping up appearances, each attack was an insult to the image of British control and this made acting on any dissention essential. Bose left for Japan after several revolutionary leaders were arrested and some executed, although he continued to fight for Indian independence from Japan and was to re-emerge later.

The decision to join the Germans during the war by the Sultan of Turkey also caused Muslim unrest, as the Turks issued five fatwahs, or rulings, in one month calling for Indians to rise up in Jihad against the British, which encouraged nationalist agitation. Because of the fatwahs, Pathans in the 130th Baluch regiment mutinied in Rangoon, Burma but they were clearly already unhappy with their lot as they had previously bayoneted a British officer when war broke out and they were posted to East Africa. As a result, 190 men were court martialled, one Indian officer and one havildar (sergeant) were shot and the rest were transported to the Andaman Islands, 1370km from the Indian mainland. In Singapore too, soldiers of the 5th Light Infantry broke out of barracks at night and killed every European they could find. The mutiny was suppressed but not before thirty-two Europeans were murdered. Authorities hanged Kasim Ismail Mansur, the Muslim tea shop owner who had spread pro-Turkish propaganda among the Singapore troops, and forty-six mutineers were executed with more imprisoned. After Turkey joined the war, other Muslims deserted, often fleeing to Afghanistan. Muslims that deserted in French battlefields were also sent to Afghanistan by the Germans. To prevent defection on the frontier, two of the Indian divisions with predominantly Muslim soldiers stationed there were swapped with units consisting of other faiths.

The Punjab also saw civil unrest in the early decades of the twentieth century and the Raj's response was swift and often severe. There was a Sikh rising in the countryside, although this was mostly directed at Hindi creditors and landlords and there were also separate Muslim peasant risings in the Punjab in Multan, Muzaffargarh and Jhang. The Hindu fundamentalist college professor Bhai Perma Nad was behind an incident in Lahore in March 1915; he was arrested and sentenced to death. From February 1915, groups of Muslim students began to disappear from Lahore, Rawalpindi and Peshawar, and started to make their way to Kabul too; at least one of these groups was shot. The government censored newspapers and closed radical press in an attempt to stop anti-Raj feelings circulating and spreading. In June 1915, the Viceroy also confined brothers Shaukat Ali and Mohamed Ali, the main Indian leaders of the pan-Islamic Khilafat Movement, to their villages, which helped quiet unrest, although it could be argued that the heavy-handed approach was fatal in the long run. Many might argue that the rebellion was merely stifled, ready to be brought back to life, in a different manner by leaders such as Gandhi.

The heavy-handed methods used by the Raj to put down detractors were made possible by the Defence of India Act passed in March 1915 despite the generally liberal outlook of Viceroy Hardinge. This was an emergency criminal law designed to curtail any nationalist and revolutionary activities during and after the First World War, using rigid, authoritarian measures to keep order, which included a ban on nationalist magazines and worked to prevent reactionary politicians from entering the Punjab. The Act gave national and provincial authorities powers of surveillance, search, arrest and internment. While such measures were at odds with much of the progress towards Indian involvement the reformist British government had made, it demonstrates that the administration was still sending mixed messages with regards to its ultimate plans. Both within the Raj and back home in Britain, a broad spectrum of views on how best to manage the colonies were still in existence.

The Act and the harsh treatment of rebels it sought to deal with did, on the surface at least, have the desired effect. Outrages dropped from twenty-four in 1916, to eight in 1917 and to six in 1918 and by August 1915 even the Ghadr revolt was stamped out, with 212 Gadhr members in Lahore charged, thirty-six sentenced to death, seventy-seven destined for transportation and fifteen imprisoned. Over 1,500 Ghadr members who had arrived from America were temporarily restricted to their villages, but for the vast majority (over 6,000) no action was taken, although they were kept under surveillance. Its leaders fled abroad, Bose to Japan, many to Afghanistan. Just as it had during the Mutiny, the sharp and swift reaction to rebels had worked. This set a dangerous precedent of course; just two years later, the same approach failed to work. Times had changed by then – but the psyche of army officers, it seems, hadn't.

While rebellion may have been put down temporarily, the experience of dealing with terror attacks reminded many in the Raj of the fears that had never really been assuaged after the Mutiny of 1857. There was now, more than ever, a feeling that it was wise for the military and civil servants to look over their shoulders and be wary about trusting natives. It must have become obvious that nationalism was making continued headway and that it would not be suppressed forever. The events in Amritsar clearly show that it was inevitable the two sides would eventually clash, and the handling of the call for independence would speak volumes about those involved. The ill-conceived Rowlatt bills were to be the catalyst for what came next.

Perhaps the biggest irony about the Rowlatt bill proposals is that it was the sentiment behind them rather than the bills themselves that led to controversy. Of the two acts submitted, eventually only one became law, which was repealed in 1922 and the provisions of which were never used or needed. Unfortunately, the chain of events that they led to ended in bloodshed and shame, galvanising the nationalist movement in a way no rebellious leader had ever managed. The minor Rowlatt bill was never enacted but was designed to increase the severity of punishment for sedition, including longer sentences for those found guilty and fines for possessing seditious literature. It also allowed for earlier convictions and associations to be brought up in court and proposed that upon release from prison, those convicted under it had to execute a bond for good behavior and keep police updated on their home address. The second bill, the Anarchical and Revolutionary Crimes Act of 1919, was passed by the Imperial Legislative Council in Delhi on 18 March and became known as the Rowlatt Act. It attempted to extend the emergency wartime measures provided for by the 1915 Defence of India Act.

The draconian measures it allowed included a court's right to stay 'in camera', enabling proceedings to be carried out away from the public and press. Evidence that would not usually be admissible now would be, there would be three judges for a case rather than a jury and no preliminary proceedings for committal. Part 2 of the Act meant suspects (rather than those actually convicted) could be forced to place a bond against good behaviour, to notify their residence to police, to abstain from any act ordered by the court and report to police when asked. The act also allowed arrest and search without a warrant and confinement without trial for up to a year which could also be renewed, meaning that a suspect could be held indefinitely without a conviction. The Rowlatt Act was a step back from the previous government moves to include Indians in administration and was a slap in the face after India's loyalty throughout the war. When the minor act was debated in the Imperial Legislative Council, every Indian member voted against it and the initial publication of the bills aroused unprecedented public opposition. All sections of society and all political persuasions were horrified, and to many it suggested that Britain had no – and never did have any – intention of gradually allowing India its freedom. Instead, the bills demonstrated that the British still didn't trust or value the Indian people and that nothing had changed since the Mutiny. While the government of India thought the acts would help them stay in control – and be seen to be just that – it was simply the case it increased hostility and fear between the Raj and those it governed.

Unfortunately, the Indian government made no effort to ease the tension and did not spend any time responding to the concern expressed. Instead, rumours began to circulate about what the natives referred to as the 'Black Act'. This included reports that police would arrest those walking in groups of two or three people, that there would be a tax on weddings and funerals, and that crops would be seized. The masses were now outraged and looked to those that could express their feelings. The consternation helped to bind together the many political groups fighting for a greater say in India's administration from those seeking home rule to those demanding complete independence. And the person who was most able to do that was Gandhi, who was also horrified at the seeming change in attitude since the Montagu reforms. He said of the Act, 'When the Rowlatt Bills were published, I felt that they were so restrictive of human liberty that they must be resisted to the utmost'. Gandhi asked the people to peacefully disobey the laws.

Two things worried the British about political agitation over the Rowlatt Act, firstly that the various strands of nationalist groups – whichever religion and strata of society they represented – began to work together and also, that they had never had to face nationwide civil disobedience before. Without a central unit to deal with such protests, each of the local governments was left to deal with rebellion as they saw fit. The result of that approach in the Punjab was disastrous.

The national *hartal* called on March 30 was peacefully observed in Amritsar. Crowds in excess of 25,000 gathered in the Jallianwala Bagh without incident (this time). In advance of the next strike however, more troops were put on standby to protect the railway.

With Hindus and Muslims marching together, and a Hindu politician welcomed into a mosque to speak in the city, the fear that Gandhi was uniting all sections of society against the Raj motivated the Punjab authorities to ban him from visiting and speaking to supporters in Amritsar. Accordingly, Gandhi was taken off a train and arrested on his way to Amritsar, which led to violent rioting across the country. In Amritsar the secret deportation of nationalist leaders Satya Pal and Kitchlew on 10 April and the ensuing protest turned violent when a military picket shot at the angry crowd.

This was the prelude to the Amritsar massacre itself of course, but also a significant point in the development of the Indian nationalist movement with many moderates no longer interested in anything other than a fully free India. This heavy-handed approach to dissention, the idea that Indian civilians were of so little value that they could be so mercilessly slaughtered without reprisals and the lack of compassion shown to the wounded and dying proved beyond doubt that the British could not be trusted. The massacre was widely condemned by political leaders; Jinnah called it 'physical butchery', while Congress issued a statement condemning the incident as 'an act without parallel in modern times'. Gandhi demanded a government investigation, threatening *satyagraha* if one was not forthcoming.

While the Amritsar massacre and the ensuing period of martial law was enough to pit Indians against British rule like never before, the way that the incident and those responsible were handled both immediately afterwards and in the longer term simply added to the increasing fury against the Raj. The British Indian press exalted Dyer, and the authorities refused to punish him appropriately. A group of British ladies even clubbed together to raise funds for a thank you gift. The Raj government also quickly passed the 'Indemnity Bill', which would protect any officials involved in the shootings and the period of martial law that followed. While the families of British victims of the violence in Amritsar were compensated generously, those natives that had suffered a loss received a paltry figure in comparison. The events solidified national support for Indian independence – and worse was to come.

In Autumn 1919, after much public pressure, the Hunter Commission began its investigation in the shooting in the Jallianwala Bagh and the behaviour exhibited by the British army while martial law was imposed immediately afterwards. The Hunter Report was published on 3 May 1920, and described the massacre as an error, said martial law was justified and decided not to formally punish Dyer or Lieutenant Governor of the Punjab, Sir Michael O'Dwyer. The findings proved unsatisfactory for many with even the Indian members of the Committee rejecting the majority opinion and creating their own minority report instead. The Hunter Committee had listened only to accounts provided by white military men and British civil servants and the investigation was quite aptly criticised for being a 'whitewash'.

Planning to set up their own report on the shooting, Congress amassed lots of evidence but had no idea how to organise it. However, Gandhi, with his keen lawyer's eye for detail and an energy none could match was able to take on the task. He created a 200-page conclusion condemning the events in the Punjab and blamed the Viceroy for not investigating. For Gandhi it was a pivotal moment and he would now become a central figure in Indian's independence movement.

Despite many politicians in Britain pushing for harsher treatment after the Hunter Report – and calling for Dyer's sacking – both Dyer and O'Dwyer escaped formal punishment. The debates in the British parliament also largely supported taking no further action. For many like Motilal and Gandhi, the shooting itself was bad enough but the whitewashed Hunter report and the lack of punishment for those responsible was the final straw and Amritsar became their political turning point.

After the events of 1919, the change in public mood following the Hunter Report and the introduction of the Montagu-Chelmsford reforms, Indian independence seemed inevitable. Hardliners like Churchill still fought any signs of an independent India, living in the past. Churchill would go on to become a member of the India Defence League, a pressure group formed in June 1933, dedicated to keeping India within the Empire. It eventually had over 100 peers as members. It was similar in vein to the Indian Empire Society, founded three years earlier, which boasted members such as O'Dwyer and other former members of the Indian Civil Service. The society was dedicated to resisting constitutional reform in India, on the premise that it feared for the fate of the Indian masses under self-rule.

However, the Montagu–Chelmsford Reforms had put in place the provision for a commission to be sent to India after ten years to examine the effects and operations of the constitutional changes and to suggest more improvements for India. Accordingly, in November 1927, the British government appointed the Indian Statutory Commission, commonly referred to as the Simon Commission. A group of seven British MPs, under the chairmanship of Sir John Allsebrook Simon, arrived in British India in 1928 to study constitutional reform. One of its members was Clement Attlee, who supported Indian independence and later would grant it as Prime Minister in 1947. At the time however, the Commission met strong opposition by many in India and encountered protests in every major Indian city it visited. Prominent Indian nationalist Lala Lajpat Rai led a protest in Lahore, during which he suffered a police beating and died of his injuries two weeks later.

It was this lack of progress and cohesion that prompted Gandhi to leave his ashram Sabarmati and step back in to politics. The sticking point was that Indians wanted independence, after which they would form a constitution, but the British insisted that the constitution must come first. It would be the Viceroy Lord Irwin who would work with nationalists to break this impasse; Irwin saw his role as that of helping the inevitable transfer of power from the Raj to India and Indians, the antithesis to so many that had gone before him. Irwin and Gandhi would go on to shape the future of an independent India. On 5 March 1931, the two men signed the Gandhi-Irwin Pact, a political agreement reached ahead of the second of three Round Table Conferences in London. Still, those against Indian independence, both in India and Britain, were outraged by the participation in the talks by the Indian National Congress, because its purpose was the 'destruction' of the British Raj. Shrewdly, however, the Labour government knew that without the presence of Gandhi and the Congress, the process would not carry much weight. Finally, Indian nationalists sat with British administrators to talk about independence.

The Government of India Act was finally introduced in 1935, and it was the largest piece of legislation in the history of the British parliament. It provided for full responsible government at the provincial level, with elections to be held as soon as possible, with those elected taking control. It also allowed for the establishment of a 'Federation of India', to be made up of both British India and some or all of the princely states and introduced direct elections, dramatically increasing the electorate from seven million to thirty-five million people. Certain areas were also split – including Burma being split from India entirely – and a federal court was established. The Act was widely criticised for appearing to offer more than it actually did. Both the Indian National Congress and the Muslim League opposed the Act but did in the end participate in the following provincial elections in 1936 and 1937. The results of these elections were to prove to the Muslim League that it was unlikely to gain a majority, and to Congress that it had gained the upper hand in representation. As the elections raised concerns that a Hindu majority might eventually rule over Muslims, there was increasing support for a separate nation altogether – Pakistan – a resolution on which was decided at a 1940 Muslim League session.

When the Second World War broke out, there were broader issues to consider than Indian independence. Nationalists had to decide if working with the British to defeat fascism was more important than the struggle for self rule. The philosophy of non-violence was also called into question; it had worked so effectively for the nationalist struggle but could it be used during wartime? Britain did not do itself any favours though as it announced India's participation in the war on its behalf and without consultation, a move that proved to Congress and nationalists generally that Britain would never see India as an equal. The period proved difficult for Gandhi and Congress as they grappled with how best to proceed and still stick to their varying nationalist principles.

It was also a challenging time for the British government, desperate to have India's support but reluctant to make too many promises about independence after the war. This led to Sir Stafford Cripps, a member of the War Cabinet, being sent to India with new proposals. Ultimately the 'Cripps Mission' failed, as neither the League nor Congress would accept it, Prime Minister Winston Churchill also rejected the proposals. For Congress, this was the end of the road for any co-operation with the British Government and instead it began the Quit India movement, launched at the Bombay session of the All India Congress Committee by Gandhi. Within hours of Gandhi delivering a speech that advocated refusal to cooperate in the war effort, almost the entire leadership of Congress was imprisoned. The Muslim League, however, agreed to continue to support the Allies, allowing them to find favour and this approach by Muhammad Ali Jinnah, the leader of the League, led to large numbers of Muslims cooperating with the British and enlisting in the army. The concept of Pakistan became a real possibility.

At the end of the war, Britain made good on its promises. Five weeks after Germany's surrender, the Viceroy, Lord Wavell, broadcast proposals for Indian independence. The first step was a conference in Simla, with Congress (whose leaders were released from prison) and the League. It was unsuccessful, and the two Indian parties could not agree. Back in England, the new Labour Attlee government wanted to honour the commitment for a free India and to cut costs; running India wasn't cheap. Fresh elections were held, more British intervention failed and eventually violence ensued. In February 1947, Lord Mountbatten took over the viceroyalty with strict instructions to transfer power by June 1948. Partition became inevitable and the two states were to gain their freedom by 15 August 1947. After all this time, the nationalists achieved their aim – the British Raj would end. The ultimate goal had been achieved but it came at the price of permanent partition and bloodshed.

Chapter 11

Gandhi and Nationalism

Mohandas Karamchand Gandhi was born into British India in 1869, in the seaside town of Porbander in Gujarat Province. His parents could be considered Liberal, since they had friends from all religions. Gandhi's father served as the Prime Minister of the Porbander and Rajkot princely states, while his mother was a devout Vaishnava Hindu and observed rigorous fasts. It's clear that these two threads of his upbringing served him well later as he combined the two disciplines to encourage millions of Indians to fight against the British Raj without hatred or violence. He received a Western education in a school in Rajkot, being taught in English. His family observed cultural traditions however and his arranged marriage took place when he was thirteen. Even at an early age, Gandhi questioned rules and broke with convention, when at nineteen he become the first in his family to leave India to study law in London, despite Hindu rules forbidding overseas travel. It caused uproar within his Modh Bania caste, but Gandhi was keen to fulfill his father's dying wish and make a success of himself and his family name.

London made quite an impression on Gandhi, as it provided him with access to social reformers and great thinkers, but he eventually rejected the British customs and clothes he briefly adopted while there as a matter of principle. The 'New Age' thinkers he befriended also helped to ignite his spirituality and strengthen his resolve in vegetarianism. Gandhi lived frugally while in England and studied hard, graduating from the Inner Temple in June 1891, returning to India to set up as a barrister, a prospect that seemed lacking in attraction after the spiritual and cultural awakening he had experienced overseas. But two years later he was to travel to Durban in South Africa to assist an Indian firm there. The move changed the course of his life and in turn history, although at the time it simply seemed a great alternative to the boredom of small town India he now faced. At the time, South Africa was in the grip of 'gold fever' and nations and individuals were all after a slice of the pie. Some Indian immigrants had done well in business, but many were not as fortunate. Many of the poorer Indians that lived there, the majority of whom came from Southern India, were in effect slaves with few rights, living in shantytowns trying to earn their freedom through their labour, often borrowing money at exorbitant lending rates. Racism in South Africa was endemic at the time; Gandhi himself was thrown off a train by police for refusing to move from a first class carriage when white passengers objected to him travelling with them because of the colour of his skin. He was also barred from sitting inside a stagecoach, having to take an outside seat usually left for the black African servant, refused a room at a hotel and a table in a dining room.

In the Orange Free State, ruled at the time by the Boers (Dutch), racism was so much the norm that Indians were only allowed to perform underpaid jobs, while in the Transvaal area (also under Dutch authority) the administration levied a £3 tax on Indians, and also forbade them to own land, vote or go out without first obtaining a permit. Gandhi lived in Natal, a British Colony, which in 1984 attempted to introduce a £2 10s tax on Indians and planned to remove their voting rights. In May that year, Gandhi changed his plans to return to India after his case had finished, and instead decided to stay in South Africa to help organise protests against the injustice he saw dished out to his people. Gandhi created the Natal Indian Congress in 1894 with some like-minded reformers, writing two pamphlets designed to raise awareness of Indian issues. A pamphlet distributed in India in 1896 while he was there to seek out Indian political support for the campaign in South Africa got him in trouble however. When he returned to Durban the following year, the authorities kept the boat on which he arrived on in quarantine and when its occupants were finally able to disembark, Gandhi was met by an enraged white mob. That evening his home was besieged and the crowds outside threatened to hang him because of what he had written about the prejudice faced by Indians in South Africa. It's at this stage that Gandhi began to practice nonviolence as a means of resistance, refusing to meet his detractors with violence or pursue them through the courts.

When the Second Anglo-Boer War broke out, Gandhi chose to work with the British, providing an ambulance corps of over 1,000 men for the wounded and was awarded a medal for his efforts. Conflict between the Boers and Britain was nothing new, there had been problems for over a century. It was a long and bloody war but British military strength eventually proved superior. During this time, Winston Churchill travelled to South Africa as a journalist attached to the Army, ending up a prisoner of war just outside of Pretoria, although he managed to escape his captors affording him plenty of admiration and fame. He was also present when Gandhi, working as a stretcher bearer, carried an injured general past him. Gandhi hoped that working alongside the British during the war would mean greater respect and equality once it was over. He was disappointed however when Transvaal authorities continued to enforce anti-Indian regulations in 1902. Gandhi went on to lead mass protests and develop the *satyagraha* philosophy of peaceful protest to object to such injustices.

Gandhi was still in South Africa when the Zulu rebellion broke out and again he offered his support and that of his volunteer ambulance unit. Britain dealt with its dissenters particularly brutally, which did not go unnoticed. When, in 1906, authorities decided to fingerprint every Indian, Gandhi mobilised his supporters, demanding they refuse, and so began Gandhi's first campaign using passive resistance. He also visited the British Colonial Office in London to seek British justice for the Indian British subjects in South Africa. There he was to meet Winston Churchill to ask if the Colonial Office would intervene and was successful in theory, although when Transvaal won self-rule just a few months later, it put in place fingerprinting and registering restrictions and the British government did not prevent it from doing so. Gandhi and his peers felt cheated, and that the British sense of fairness that they had so much admired had failed them. Churchill had simply hoped to shift the responsibility from his shoulders to those of the new Transvaal Parliament, while achieving his ultimate aim, to preserve South Africa as part of the British Empire at any cost. As a result, Gandhi realised that if he wanted to change things, he would need to put into practice the civil disobedience philosophy he had been working on – passive resistance – or *satyagraha*, as he called it. Marches, pickets and speeches were arranged and Gandhi asked Indians to refuse to cooperate with the fingerprinting scheme. Eventually, one man was sent to prison for entering the region with an expired registration certificate, but after his release rather than face further action, he fled. Gandhi was told to leave the country and jailed when he ignored the order, and over 2,000 of his supporters faced the same fate. The movement was floundering and Gandhi agreed a compromise – that Indians should voluntarily allow fingerprinting – in his mind very different from being compelled to do so. Many of his supporters did not agree and felt betrayed and angry. By 1908, Gandhi had been released from prison and begun to build up support again, but when he organised a mass burning of registration papers he found himself behind bars again and many Indians instead decided to register rather than risk their freedom and livelihood. He would spend a further term in jail in 1909 before finding that his views had become unpopular, and he instead went to London to the Colonial Office to seek support, hopeless though the case seemed.

In London, Gandhi's ideas clashed with the nationalist movements of the time – namely those run by Vinayak Savarkar out of India House – which glorified violence and terror. If such people won freedom for India, how would they rule it? Gandhi worried. If you use the imperial methods of violence to be rid of the British, you simply recreate a greedy, morally bankrupt community to replace them, he reasoned. He was invited to a banquet with Indian nationalists, and sympathisers of Savarkar, and spoke about his alternative approach. Gandhi now decided his best work would be achieved by changing the approach of the nationalist movement to an ethical one that Indians could be proud of. Gandhi drew strength and inspiration from Westerners who also wanted to see India free, from British writer G.K. Chesterton, who thought India should be free to become Indian rather than a poor imitation of Westernised power and government to Russian aristocrat Leo Tolstoy, who argued Indians should simply refuse to participate in the Raj. Gandhi drew up a fifteen-point Confession of Faith, in which he wanted a new India to reject the Western influences such as engineering, modern medical practices and communication technologies, instead living a simple, peasant life to find true happiness.

Soon after, he created his manifesto *Hind Swaraj* (Indian self-rule), outlining a path to freedom that encouraged Indians to go back to their roots as an ancient civilization of peace and honour. Gandhi urged Indians to chose good conduct and simplicity, and to rethink the way it was common to treat the lower-caste Indians in their society. He also proposed *satyagraha,* the soul force (rather than brute force) necessary to achieve freedom, using peaceful methods of protest, such as the boycott of British goods, and choosing traditional Indian cloth over imported British clothes. The British Government knew the call for resistance on a massive scale, if successful, could prove problematic. Consequently, his book was banned in India.

In March 1913, Gandhi was to embark on his final tussle with the South African government. The authorities had ruled that Indians married according to religious rites that recognized polygamy had no right to emigrate to South Africa, even if they had a monogamous marriage. This decision coupled with ever-tightening restrictions of immigration to and within South Africa for Indians would give rise to Gandhi's fourth *satyagraha* campaign. He asked his wife and friends to break the regulations preventing Indians from crossing from Natal into Transvaal. They were caught and sentenced to three months hard labour. He then appealed to the indentured Indians in South Africa, who he had previously not considered or approached. These people were trapped in a cycle of debt and servitude and a tax requirement was likely to mean their children would follow in their footsteps. Gandhi called for a strike in protest at the tax and the response was staggering. Within a fortnight, 5,000 mine workers were on strike and Gandhi organised for them to march across the border in unity. The government deliberately did not intervene, not wishing to hand Gandhi martyrs to the cause. Instead they arrested only him, hoping that the miners would dwindle without a leader. Gandhi was released simply to reoffend, and then receive a sentence of three-months hard labour. Returned to their jobs, the miners however refused to work at all and rebellion spread to Natal and sugar plantations by the coast, paralyzing many industries. International sympathy was with the Indian labourers in South Africa and the government there was forced to negotiate. The tax was abolished and the marriage rights of Hindus and Muslims were recognised. The registration and immigration laws however remained untouched. Gandhi had won some concessions though not all, but he had proved *satyagraha* could work.

With war in Europe declared in 1914, Gandhi docked in England on his way back to India. He helped the best way he knew how, by organising an Indian ambulance corps for the British, despite his views on the Empire. But the weather and his health got the better of him and in 1915 he returned to a warm welcome arriving in Bombay's Apollo Bunder quay, normally reserved for the Viceroy or royalty. He began travelling around the country to see and meet for himself the citizens whom he wanted to help. He wore a traditional loincloth, travelled third class and learnt Indian languages other than his own. At the time, Indian nationalism was centred on the Indian National Congress and two of its leaders, Gopal Krishna Gokhale and B.G. Tilak. Tilak had supported extremist views, eventually causing him to be expelled from the Congress, leaving moderate Gokhale at the forefront. Gokhale sought home rule in partnership with Britain. Gandhi also set up the Sabarmati Ashram, and as well as extended family and those from his earlier ashrams, he invited an untouchable husband and wife to live there as an illustration of his beliefs.

In 1916, Gandhi had been asked to speak at the opening of a university, attended by the Viceroy and the Maharaja of Darbhanga. He took this opportunity to speak his mind, firstly criticising the use of English at such events, then the state of local hygiene, the riches on display by guests that could instead be used to feed the poor and the use of bodyguards to protect Viceroy Hardinge. Before he could be ushered off the stage, Gandhi railed against his nation's surrender to British rule, claiming that if Indians want self rule, they would have to take it. This speech burned bridges for Gandhi and sidelined him from nationalist movements.

At ground level, however, Gandhi was making an impact. In 1917, he successfully led a protest against British landlords in Bihar, Eastern India who were forcing the peasants to cultivate indigo for a fixed price rather than food crops, and pay high taxes, despite a famine. Gandhi also obtained a pay rise for mill workers in Ahmedabad, the second largest city in the Bombay region. The flourishing cotton industry had meant that the city became a modern industrial town but the mill owners wanted to withdraw a bonus payment from its workers. Gandhi organised a political fast and the workers went on to receive a wage rise. In 1918, he led a further *satyagraha* for the peasants of Kheda in support of an unrealistic tax increase in the region.

The Raj was aware of his movements and his motives, and for this reason they let him go about his business despite considering expulsion, fearing that any action would turn Gandhi into a martyr and allow him to mobilise support from the masses. The Indian government was between a rock and a hard place, because while their inaction may have prevented riots, it also led to Gandhi's supporters feeling victorious, affording him popularist leader status and proving his methods worked. His peaceful approach also meant that authorities preferred to negotiate with him rather than with other less obliging Indian leaders. As Gandhi came to the fore however, other nationalist leaders and groups lost popularity, not least Annie Besant. Gandhi was even invited to attend the Delhi War Conference at the government's request in April 1918 and, controversially for a pacifist, agreed to help recruit Indians for the war hoping that becoming a soldier would teach men about self-sacrifice and bravery, readying them for an independent India. Gandhi was awarded the Kaiser-I-Hind medal for this support. When the First World War came, Gandhi was happy to support the British, believing that, in the culture of fairness, Britain would reward Indian loyalty with negotiations for self-government. He was wrong.

As the war dragged on, hardships across the Empire increased and the British government worried that the loss of Indian troops and increased cost of living would threaten the loyalty of its subjects in India. In a move that some might regard as a calculating enticement to continue to support the war effort, Edwin Montagu, the Secretary of State for India announced a programme that would see more native inclusion in government. Many nationalists assumed this change would mean that self-government was closer than ever and tussled over who would take charge; even the Lucknow Pact collapsed. Disagreements caused riots in Bihar, shocking the administration. When the government finally announced further details, it had modified the plans to facilitate a dyarchy that ensured central government control remained with the Viceroy, and that only the less crucial functions such as agriculture and education were passed to Indian ministers. The Indian National Congress and other nationalists were outraged.

But it was the creation of the Rowlatt Acts that was to force Gandhi to pick up the mantle for nationalists. When the British introduced the single Rowlatt Act in 1919 Gandhi knew it was time to protest. The law severely limited the political freedom of Indians and pushed Gandhi into the spotlight as a leader of a national campaign of strikes and passive resistance. While these campaigns were not a massive success, the government was worried enough about Gandhi's popularity to prevent him from visiting Amritsar where a mass demonstration was planned. News of Gandhi's removal from a train triggered riots in Bombay and Ahmedabad. The worst violence was to be witnessed in Amritsar, lighting the touch paper that would ignite Reginald Dyer to commit his infamous atrocity.

For Gandhi the Jallianwala Bagh massacre, the consequent martial law and the failure of the British and Indian Governments to appropriately punish Dyer was the final straw. He lost all faith in the British Empire and abandoned the idea of self-governance under a foreign ruler. He now wanted only full Indian independence. Having worked on the eyewitness evidence that Congress gathered, Gandhi felt utterly cheated when the Viceroy accepted the Hunter Report findings and chose not to punish Dyer or O'Dwyer further. It was a turning point for Gandhi, and he decided to work within mainstream national politics; it also made him reconsider his loyalty to the British Empire.

In April 1920, he replaced Annie Besant as President of the All-India Home Rule League, then he took a prominent role at the All India Congress Committee meeting in Benares, which rejected the Hunter Report as 'tainted with racial bias'. By 1 August 1920, Gandhi had returned his South Africa War and Kaiser-i-Hind medals to Viceroy Chelmsford with a note that explained he was no longer loyal to the Empire. A few days later he would launch a *satyagraha* campaign in support of the Khilafat Movement that voiced Muslim outrage against the British government's anti-Turkey policy, hoping that it would bring Hindu-Muslim unity. One of Gandhi's main aims was to unite the two religions and he was devastated by the sectarian violence that followed Partition.

India's Muslims had felt vulnerable and outnumbered in India, with the majority of Muslims living in rural and poorer areas and being less well represented in local government and civil service. With war waged on the Khalifa and the Indian government working with Hindus they felt even more threatened. But Gandhi understood the importance of Hindu-Muslim unity, not least because of its importance in South African campaigns. He taught that his peers were Indian first, and Hindus, Muslim, Parsi, Christian second – that if an issue mattered to Indian Muslims, then it must matter to all other Indians.

Gandhi fully outlined his plans to oppose the Raj at a special session called by the Indian National Congress in September 1920. He wanted waves of protest, starting with a mass return of honorary British titles, positions, awards, memberships and the like. He asked that no one stand for upcoming legislative elections for the new councils drawn up by the Montagu-Chelmsford reforms and for teachers, children and students to walk out from government-supported schools and colleges across the nation. Next, lawyers and judges were to boycott the British courts, and then came a refusal to buy anything but Indian-made goods. The final moves were to withdraw from serving in the police and army and to never pay taxes to the Raj again. It was the 'progressive non-violent non-cooperation' plan outlined in his *Hind Swaraj*, and a total shutdown of the Raj, and he believed it would result in a spiritual liberation of India.

Motilal Nehru, C.R. Das and Vallabhbhai Patel (popularly known as Sardar Patel, he would go on to become the first Deputy Prime Minister of India) followed Gandhi's suggestion and quit their law practices and the British courts. Subhas Chandra Bose also resigned from the Indian Civil Service but would later quarrel with Gandhi and go on to work with the Germans during the Second World War. Gandhi promised those at the session that if his plan were followed, Swaraj would be achieved within a year. The membership voted and Gandhi won by a narrow majority, and his plan was turned into a Resolution at the next full Congress meeting. Gandhi helped to write a new constitution for Congress and insisted local languages were used instead of English at future meetings. It was now a truly national and nationalist movement.

Gandhi's idea of non-cooperation had its ups and downs, with protests getting out of control in 1920 and in 1921 when the Prince of Wales visited India. In 1922, a protest in Chauri Chaura ended in violence, ten days after which Gandhi halted the non-cooperation *satyagraha*. Many of those already imprisoned felt betrayed by Gandhi's about face and the decision to stop led to suspicion from his Muslim allies, who eventually deserted him altogether. Back in England, the chaos was used by Churchill to show how Liberal policies had caused more not less trouble and that self-rule was not practical. As Secretary of State, Montagu sought reassurance from Prime Minister Lloyd George that British policy was still to work towards the long-term goal of a self-governing India. Lloyd George was to disappoint Montagu, deciding that India still needed its British master. Churchill was delighted, Montagu resigned.

Gandhi took responsibility for the trouble the protests had caused and was sentenced to six years imprisonment. He was released after two years due to ill health – the British did not want him to die a martyr in jail. He continued to work on achieving *poorna swaraj* (complete independence), uniting Hindu and Muslim factions in society and reducing discrimination against those from the 'untouchable' castes. His work also led him to embark on the historic march to Dandi in Gujarat, where he lifted a symbolic fistful of salt in defiance of laws that allowed only the British to harvest and sell the mineral. The salt tax was a government monopoly dating back to Mughal times and was a symbol of India's subjection. Everyone paid the tax – rich or poor. Gandhi was arrested for his defiance, but thousands joined the protest, making salt, striking and picketing foreign goods. Many thousands were arrested too – some violently beaten by police – but in February 1931, Gandhi was released and signed a pact with Viceroy Lord Irwin to release the salt march prisoners, allow civil protests, lift a ban on the Congress party and to permit people in coastal towns to make their own salt.

The Congress party hoped to use the Second World War as a chance to exchange their support for Indian independence, but the British administration ignored the opportunity. By early 1942 however, the British were prepared to negotiate and sent Sir Stafford Cripps to discuss the future. The talks broke down and by July Gandhi had formulated his 'Quit India' campaign, supported by Congress but opposed by the Muslim League. Gandhi announced the movement during a speech in Bombay causing widespread strikes and demonstrations. The next day Gandhi and other Congress leaders were arrested, causing violent clashes between supporters and the government, with the police being accountable for 10,000 deaths.

The next major hurdle for independence and peace in India was the demand by the Muslim League for a separate Muslim state, a concept with which Gandhi did not agree. However, the legislative councils of the Punjab and Bengal voted in favour of partition. Borders were drawn on the northwest and northeast of British India and a mass exodus of people begun as Sikhs, Hindus and Muslims moved to the side of the border they wanted to live within. This chaos caused riots and killings. Pakistan came into being on 14 August 1947 and India gained its independence the next day. Gandhi however did not celebrate, spending the day fasting and in prayer, mourning the communal unrest caused by partition. Winston Churchill told the House of Commons that 'at least 400,000 men and women have slaughtered each other in the Punjab alone' – which he pointed out was more than all the losses of the British Empire in the Second World War.

Less than six months later, Gandhi was shot dead at point-blank range by the right-wing Hindu nationalist, Nathuram Godse. The shocking news of his assignation stopped much of the violence around India with over two million people attending his funeral procession in Delhi. Gandhi became known as the 'Father of the Nation' and has inspired many other world leaders and activists to achieve positive change through non-violent means. And the Amritsar massacre had played a key role in shaping Gandhi's philosophies and aims.

Chapter 12

Who is to Blame for the Jallianwala Bagh Shooting?

When discussing the Amritsar Massacre, much of the emphasis is placed on Reginald Dyer, both as a person and as a soldier. Can just one man really be to blame for such an atrocity? It's true that Dyer was in charge of the city at the time, that he planned the attack in the hours between his procession through the city earlier in the day and his march to the Jallianwala Bagh and that ultimately he gave the order to fire, including where to aim the bullets and the duration of the shooting. It's also clear to see that he was a product of his upbringing, the era he lived in and his own, often harsh, life experiences. But while Dyer can be held culpable, the Jallianwala Bagh incident could not have happened without many preceding events and the decisions taken by others who should also be subject to censure.

Sir Michael O'Dwyer for example, had been Lieutenant Governor of the Punjab since 1912, and when he was given the role the then Viceroy Lord Hardinge warned that the region was a difficult one – likely to explode. Knighted in 1913 and awarded the Most Eminent Order of the Indian Empire four years later, at the age of 75 however, O'Dwyer was shot dead by Indian revolutionary Udham Singh in a revenge attack for the Jallianwala Bagh. Singh had witnessed the events and been injured at the Bagh and he held O'Dwyer responsible for the massacre. And Singh is not alone for laying the blame for the Amritsar massacre at O'Dwyer's door. It was O'Dwyer that caused earlier rioting in the city by deporting Saifuddin Kitchlew and Satya Pal and ordering Gandhi be apprehended. He had previously censored and closed local press that spoke out against the government. These heavy-handed actions, designed to quell nationalism, had exactly the opposite effect and the demands for the release of their leaders caused angry mobs to turn to violence, vandalism and looting to show their anger and frustration. O'Dwyer also imposed martial law across the Punjab, even sending an aeroplane to bomb civilian rioters in Gujranwala. O'Dwyer effectively lit the fuse that caused the Punjab to detonate despite the earlier warning that the area was volatile. Singh was hanged at Pentonville Prison in 1940 for the murder of O'Dwyer, a charge to which he was happy to confess, saying, 'He deserved it. He was the real culprit. He wanted to crush the spirit of my people, so I have crushed him.' Many consider Udham Singh a martyr and in 1952, Nehru (by then Prime Minister) honoured Udham Singh, who was given the title of 'Shaheed', an Arabic word that identifies him as a hero. Singh's remains were exhumed in 1974, repatriated to India, and his ashes now rest at the Jallianwala Bagh.

As well as causing the initial unrest in the city of Amritsar that led to Dyer being sent to maintain order, O'Dwyer was happy to continue sending reinforcements and armoured vehicles to the city; clearly, he felt a show of military might was the answer to any – and all – native unrest. He also replaced the more hesitant Major MacDonald, who was in charge of Amritsar during the initial trouble, with fiery-natured Lieutenant Colonel Morgan on the say-so of hardliner Commissioner Kitchin. Perhaps more importantly however, O'Dwyer was also integral in the way the event was investigated and this is one aspect of the atrocity that has caused so much controversy. Not only was O'Dwyer slow to respond to initial reports of the mass shooting, refusing to attend the city himself despite being awoken at 3am by a concerned college principal, he held back from pushing for details from Dyer and passing information on. O'Dwyer's approval of Dyer's actions were noted in the war diary at a Government House conference the day after the Jallianwala Bagh shooting. When he had to, O'Dwyer questioned Dyer several times about the matter, and was always happy with Dyer's account despite the fact that details had changed along the way. While O'Dwyer did cancel the Crawling Order once he heard about it, at no point did he express concern over Dyer's approach and he appeared to conceal the full number of casualties from Edwin Montagu for as long as he could.

During the Hunter Committee, O'Dwyer complained about the cross examination he received from the Indian Committee members, unhappy that civilian natives were allowed to question him in this manner and continued to voice his support for Dyer. He supported the campaign that portrayed Dyer as the 'Saviour of India' for many years, desperate to clear the name of his junior officer. After the Hunter Report was published, O'Dwyer began to harass the British government, Montagu, the War Office and even the Prime Minister in an attempt to clear Dyer's name. He had open letters published in the press and successfully sued Sir C Sankaran Nair, author of *Gandhi and Anarchy* that suggested, as Dyer's superior, he was to blame for atrocities in the Punjab. O'Dwyer went on to join the India Defence League, a pressure group formed in June 1933 dedicated to keeping India within the Empire. He was an old man when he was assassinated and is remembered as describing the events in the Jallianwala Bagh as 'correct'.

There were also several men in the background, subtly stepping back as Dyer seemed to step forward. These men may have acted as advisors, egging on Dyer to take the decisive action they dared not. These include A.J.W. Kitchin, the Commissioner of Lahore, who had set up a headquarters at the city's railway station after the riots following the arrest of Satya Pal and Kitchlew. Kitchin verbally handed over control to the military when Major MacDonald arrived, who he asked to use 'all military force' to bring Amritsar to heel. Kitchin also kept in regular contact with O'Dwyer and later complained when MacDonald postponed marching through the city until after the natives had held funerals. With his regular interaction in the military operation however, it could be said he was in part responsible for the blurring of the lines of authority. Kitchin also took charge of the Deputy Commissioner, Miles Irving, who he instructed to set up the HQ at the station, and to write a proclamation banning gatherings, which was published on the morning of the 11th. Irving seems to have been ill-equipped for his role as he was happy to do exactly as his direct superior Kitchin told him, and to hand over all responsibility to the military. Irving was also responsible for the dissemination of the proclamation he wrote under orders from Kitchin, but in reality, he simply passed it on to visiting lawyers who came to negotiate the right to bury their dead. After the event, Irving was another individual who chose to send scant details of the incident to their superiors; Irving only reported 200 dead in his wire to Gerard Wathen at 11.30pm, who demanded a fuller report. Perhaps he was aware that by taking an active part in the arrests of Kitchlew and Satya Pal, he was as guilty as anyone for the unrest.

Kitchin left Amritsar to return to Lahore on the 11th and only returned after the massacre, when he continued to encourage Dyer in his use of martial law and force. Kitchin also gathered a group of leaders together on the 14th to ask them if they wanted war or peace, and then left the meeting in the charge of Dyer. Irving was also in attendance and again was happy to tell the people that it was Dyer who was in charge. During the massacre, Irving was reportedly asleep.

In 1920, the Labour Party denounced the 'cruel and barbarous' actions of British officers in the Punjab at its conference in Scarborough. It also wanted Lord Chelmsford (as well as O'Dwyer) brought to trial for his part in the treatment of natives. Could the Viceroy responsible for the creation of the Montagu-Chelmsford Reforms, designed to introduce self-governing institutions gradually to India, also be to blame for an incident widely regarded as the worst atrocity of the British Raj? The role reported directly to the Secretary of State for India in London and was one of the most powerful positions at the time, with the might of the British Indian Army at its disposal. Frederic John Napier Thesiger, the 1st Viscount Chelmsford, took up his role from 1916, succeeding Lord Hardinge. The Viceroy was the public face of the British presence in India, attending many ceremonial functions and political affairs.

But Lord Chelmsford's part in the 1919 Government of India Act (more popularly known as the Montagu-Chelmsford Reforms) was overshadowed by the passing of repressive anti-terrorism laws in the form of the Rowlatt Act. The Act gave the Viceroy certain powers, curtailing the usual legal processes and meaning provincial governments could potentially intern suspects. A response to the act was one of the items to be discussed at the fateful Jallianwala Bagh meeting on 13 April.

Chelmsford also initially supported Dyer, when Edwin Montagu learnt of the Crawling Order for example, he telegraphed Chelmsford to say Dyer should be relieved of his command. But the Viceroy did not agree, pointing to Dyer's recent success in Thal as reason enough for Dyer to stay in command. He did not visit Amritsar or the Punjab to assess the situation himself and delayed officially investigating the events for as long as he could, only eventually accepting Dyer's retirement when the Hunter Report forced his hand. Chelmsford's tardiness also gave Dyer's supporters ammunition by leaving Montagu in the dark first about the number of casualties and later by only sending a hard copy of the Report of the Disorders Enquiry Committee (India) to Montagu to arrive in London after he knew the Dyers would. If he had ever supported Montagu's ideals for an independent India, he was happy to abandon them (and his colleague) to save his own skin

And what of Edwin Montagu, the Secretary of State for India, Cabinet Minister and Political Head of the India Office, effectively in charge of the British Raj at the time? Montagu was a British Liberal, considered 'radical', with the traditional British education at University College London and Trinity College, Cambridge behind him. He was also only the third practicing Jew to serve in the Cabinet. Montagu undoubtedly supported reform in India and wanted a more considered approach when dealing with rebels. However, he had geographical distance and a time difference working against him – and some rather shifty colleagues. Nevertheless, Montagu could have prevented the Rowlatt Act being passed if he'd pressed harder and thus potentially prevented Amritsar. In his defence, he did also push for an official investigation into the event and managed to get Indian representatives on the Hunter Committee, no doubt an uphill struggle, but failed to get Chelmsford to take immediate action with Dyer.

Some suggest that Montagu foresaw the long-term problems the Jallianwala Bagh shooting would bring, which is why he worried about his part in them. Montagu chaired the Indian Disorders Committee, but found that the Army Council would not support condemnation of Dyer. He was also publicly attacked by O'Dwyer and the press and found himself open to ridicule in the House (not helped by Chelmsford deliberately keeping many of the details about Amritsar from him). He also suffered a nervous breakdown and became emotional and incoherent when questioned about the incident in the House. Montagu's political career became another casualty of Amritsar, and he died at the age of forty-five. If other people didn't blame Montagu for his part in the Jallianwala Bagh, it's likely that he did blame himself.

Another key player in the events that followed Amritsar was Winston Churchill. Born into British privilege, Churchill's father had been a well-known Tory statesman and Secretary of State for India, who became a hardline reactionary while in the colony. Churchill grew up believing that the Empire was an essential part of the British economy and personality and would go on to do everything he could to retain it. He disliked nationalists – and particularly Gandhi – but conversely was a harsh critic of Dyer. In 1919, Churchill was the Secretary of State for War, in charge of the War Office. He openly condemned Dyer in parliament, criticising his use of arms to send a message to would-be rebels, a practice that he argued contradicted the military principle of minimum force. Churchill also fought with the Military Members of the Army Council, in a bid to punish Dyer through compulsory retirement, but ultimately failed.

There may even be some weight to the argument that nationalist leaders were in part to blame for the deaths on 13 April 1919. It's likely the organisers of the political meeting knew there could be some trouble as rightly or wrongly the authorities had banned gatherings and 'seditious' activities. The meeting was well planned with many speakers arranged, and a stage for them to speak from, and there was even a man handing out water; it was not a last-minute event. The Jallianwala Bagh was a large open space and was an ideal spot for the crowds the organisers hoped to attract but it was also a place where families and pilgrims rested, some of whom may well have been unaware they were flouting the rules and being put in danger. Of course, civilians had every right to protest against the Government of India – and this meeting was designed to be peaceful – so it's hard to condemn the public for behaving as many of us would today if faced with similar persecution and lack of civil rights.

After the true nature of the Amritsar massacre and the brutality of martial law dished out across the Punjab and other regions came to the fore, India and its people were failed yet again. The Government of India resisted an investigation into the Jallianwala Bagh shooting as long as it could, despite external pressure. The Hunter Committee, while perhaps noble in conception, failed to seek out evidence from anyone but the British authorities and its members presented verdicts according to predictable race divisions. The House of Commons, the House of Lords and the Army Council in England all debated the issues raised by the problems in the Punjab, yet members refused to allow the disciplining of one of their own, especially if that meant they would have to accept the views of natives above those of a white man. Finally, the pomp and honour afforded to Dyer at his funeral in 1927 demonstrated that the opinions of the British establishment had never changed. The crowds that watched and grieved were a stark contrast to the mourners of those buried in haste after the horror of their death in the Jallianwala Bagh of Amritsar.

Despite all the failings by individuals and institutions on that day and afterwards, the ultimate blame lies of course with the government of India and therefore the British government of the time. The decision by

Dyer to open fire on the unarmed, civilian crowd – and particularly to do so without first issuing a warning and then ceasing fire once the crowd began to disperse - was a symptom of the system. A system that promoted ethnocentric racism, a system that built the myth of the paternal role of the British Empire and a system that refused to accept political change. It was the same system that refused to punish Dyer and those others involved in the brutality. And perhaps this is where the blame should lie.

Chapter 13

The Far-Reaching Effects of Amritsar

Some believe that the massacre at Amritsar was a reaction to the most widespread and successful political agitation taken against the British in India since the Mutiny of 1857. The slow and mixed, yet ultimately critical, response to the events in the Punjab by the British back in England is also considered an indication that the appetite for colonial rule was on the wane at the time. The incident is regarded as a pivotal point in Indian history and imperial politics. Apart from the devastating effect on those caught up in the violence, what longer-term impact did it have?

Dyer's brutality when he ordered his men to open fire on an unarmed and peaceful crowd of civilians in the enclosed Jallianwala Bagh – and the lack of condemnation from the Raj – consolidated Indian opinion behind the campaign for national independence. Up until now, many had accepted the idea of shared rule and dominion status, but the Amritsar massacre made even the most moderate Indian push for full freedom on the terms of India's own people. In this respect, the massacre at the Jallianwala Bagh is often considered the one incident that galvanised the nationalist movement in India, which had not always been coherent and straightforward. Severing forever relations between the British in India and the Indians they ruled over, the mass shooting dramatically increased the cross-societal support for nationalism and effectively brought about Indian independence.

Until this point, nationalism as a movement in India was far from organised and accordingly, its development was not linear but eclectic. It had encompassed ideas based on both anti-colonialism and religion-centric independence, and even a combination of these two philosophies. India of course is – and was – a huge and diverse country, so the varied movements calling for self-government were set apart geographically, culturally and linguistically, although initial nationalist organisations can mostly be traced to Calcutta, Bombay and Madras. Accordingly, many threads of co-existent nationalist thinking developed within the continent, which included those from parties as diverse as the Indian National Congress, the Muslim League, the National Liberal Federation and the Communist Party of India. Even as the Second World War became inevitable, nationalism had to detour from its ultimate aim as it decided whether to battle the British or unite to fight fascism and the possibility of an even worse invader. Should nationalists turn England's difficulties into India's opportunity or not? Again, opinion was divided.

Indian nationalism had been greatly influenced by the emergence of social groups, such as an educated elite, by the formation (and later development) of Congress in 1885 and by individuals such as Gandhi and Annie Besant. It also went through periods of militancy, extremism and violence, as leaders such as Tilak, Lajpat Rai and Bipin Chandra Pal tried to form a New Party that opposed the Congress approach of working with the British to achieve self-rule. But individual incidents also radically shaped the Indian nationalist movement – and none more so than the events at the Jallianwala Bagh on 13 April 1919. The Amritsar Massacre in fact proved to be perhaps the most significant catalyst for the demand for a free India.

Among those directly affected by Amritsar was Gandhi, who alongside Motilal Nehru, the father of Jawaharlal Nehru who would go on to be the first Prime Minister of an independent India, sifted through witness statements from the event that Congress had collected when it realised the Hunter Committee would come up wanting. Their colleague C.F. Andrews described both their shocked responses and said that the evidence 'shook the very foundations of the faith on which Motilal had built up his life'. The events had a similarly dramatic effect on Gandhi who, prior to the shooting at Amritsar, was prepared to work with the British to achieve self-rule. Such was the censorship surrounding British actions in the Punjab that Gandhi did not learn the truth about the extent of the massacre in the Jallianwala Bagh until June. When he did learn the truth, he was horrified – and would change his approach to the British Raj.

Gandhi had always perplexed the British – the philosophy outlined in his *Hind Swaraj* did not support nationalism based on hatred, while his passive resistance movement still presented them with many problems.

It was his ability to create a mass base of support for self-rule and his inclusive approach to politics however that really unnerved the Raj. The *hartals* Gandhi organised, which effectively shut down India, were a phenomenal achievement, not least because they were mostly peaceful; and coupled with that his ability to encourage Hindus and Muslims to work together, Gandhi put British traditionalists such as Dyer on edge. This new, and rapidly unfolding, challenge to the authority of the Raj in the Punjab – a region that had been so essential to the success of British rule – was clearly one of the underlying causes of the disproportionate response which Dyer and his superiors thought appropriate.

For Gandhi, the massacre and the actions carried out under the consequent period of martial law and – perhaps more importantly – the lack of censure following them, added to the disillusionment he had begun to experience with the British. Gandhi had already described the Rowlatt acts as 'immoral, unjust and arrogant beyond description' and as he worked with Congress gathering evidence on the atrocities carried out in Punjab and saw how the Caliphate was being treated, his lack of trust for the British intensified. Despite his non-violent approach, Gandhi still expressed the bitterness he felt, and described the British Empire as 'representing Satanism' and accused it of 'terrible atrocities' that it should apologise for. He returned to the Viceroy his two South African war medals and the decoration he had been awarded for humanitarian work there, describing the actions of Dyer and other officers as 'out of proportion to the crime of the people and amounted to wanton cruelty and inhumanity almost unparalleled in in modern times'. Gandhi also criticised the Viceroy for his light treatment of O'Dwyer and the British House of Lords for the way it regarded and dealt with the atrocities carried out in the Punjab, explaining that these factors had caused his estrangement from the government of India. From this point, Congress would be led by Gandhi's non-cooperation approach and the ultimate aim of self-rule, which he promised would come within a year using his method. In turn, Gandhi's ascendancy within Congress would lead to Al Jinnah's retreat from it, as he did not agree with Gandhi's philosophies. Jinnah had been dubbed the 'ambassador of Hindu-Muslim unity', holding membership of both Congress and the Muslim League, but his departure from Congress would open up an old divide, with far-reaching consequences. Muslim political leaders had long worried about living in states controlled by a Hindu majority, a paranoia, it can be argued, that stemmed from the British approach of 'divide and conquer' that segregated Indian society, encouraged infighting and thereby ensured the Raj remained in control. The desire for a separate Muslim nation – Pakistan – offered the solution to this fear and fuelled calls by the League for Partition. When the Raj relinquished its control over the continent, Partition and Indian independence became mutually dependent. As part of the deal for an independent India, the Muslim League demanded the separate Muslim territory, to be called Pakistan. The plan to divide the Empire into two new nation states was announced via the All India Radio by British Prime Minister Attlee on 3 June 1947.

And deciding upon the 3,000 miles of border between the two countries was a thankless task that fell to Sir Cyril Radcliffe. Having never been to India before, Radcliffe had just six weeks to split up the 1.8 million square mile area, taking into consideration the statistical proportion of the religious persuasion of inhabitants alongside cultural, geographical and historical factors. The Punjab region was particularly badly affected by Partition as it was divided in two, and prior to Partition, religious tensions had already started to develop. The Punjab saw the greatest violence, although riots also occurred in Delhi, Bombay, Karachi, Quetta, Varanasi, Shahjahanpur, Simla, Gujarat, Rajasthan and Nagpur. Partition created a refugee crisis as millions of people migrated to the side of the border they felt safest within. Ethnic cleansing became the method of claiming an area for one group over another. The violence could not be controlled or contained as British troops withdrew but their replacements proved ill prepared for their takeover.

Partition was to become responsible for mass displacement, bitter violence and the deaths of at least one million people. If Dyer felt his shooting at Jallianwala Bagh had spared the region and the nation bloodshed, then he was mistaken. As surely as his actions had made independence inevitable, it had also in turn forced Partition. While British rule had encouraged the racial divisions that pushed the League and Congress so far apart, the damage wrought by Amritsar and Dyer's lack of real punishment were all part of the backdrop that made this bloody separation inevitable.

Another casualty of the massacre was Edwin Montagu, Secretary of State for India, and the political party he represented. The radical Liberal had long supported constitutional reforms for India – and wanted stronger condemnation of Dyer. In the Commons debate he asked: 'Are you going to keep your hold on India by terrorism, racial humiliation, subordination and frightfulness, or are you going to rest it upon the goodwill and the growing goodwill of the people of your Indian Empire?' His question centred on Dyer's explanation that he had fired at the crowds in the Jallianwala Bagh to send a message to any potential rebels in the region. It was a crucial point in the debate, as British military guidelines only allowed minimum force to be used but Dyer meted out the punishment of some to act as a deterrent for others. Tory hardliners however were not impressed with Montagu's lack of support for Dyer, and his sympathies with Indian nationalists. He was also criticised because he seemed to lack full possession of the facts in a timely manner – when it's likely Viscount Chelmsford had deliberately concealed them.

Amritsar and the Punjab would be Montagu's downfall. Depressed and friendless after his performance in the House he resigned two years later over the partitioning of Turkey. He lost his seat in 1922 and died in 1924, with the Liberal Party never returning to govern the country as a majority.

One hundred years on, Amritsar continues to affect the relationship between Britain and India. The controversy over the act itself, and the treatment of Dyer, his superior officers and supporters, have never been laid to rest. The massacre overshadows every state visit to the continent and is regularly raised in Parliament. But as the centenary approaches, there is a chance for closure.

Chapter 14

100 Years on, Time to Say Sorry

There is no doubt that the actions of Reginald Dyer on 13 April 1919 were barbaric. He ordered the shooting of unarmed civilians who had no way to escape the bullets, and who had not been asked to leave the area prior to the command to fire. Many of the victims were in no way connected to political agitation and those who were there to organise or listen to anti-government speakers could and should have been dealt with in a far more humane manner. Dyer also left the area immediately afterwards, offering no assistance to the wounded and dying. Because of a curfew imposed by the authorities at the time, many of the injured lay there overnight without medical help, some to die in agony. Immediately after the event, martial law was imposed for several months with humiliations commonplace, including brutal marches in searing heat and floggings of everyone from schoolboys to an entire marriage party.

From today's perspective, we can little imagine how this behaviour could in any way be justified; these people were subjects of her majesty's empire – the people we claimed to protect. While the British Raj might have been facing opposition – which was sometimes violent – we were not fighting a war, simply entering a time when colonial politics was changing. And in this specific example, the event was preceded by two days of peace, in which those who supported Gandhi's non-violent philosophies sought to create open discourse rather than chaos. At the time, many British people in England were horrified and sought to investigate the matter fully. Only those within British India and the ultra-conservative upper echelons of British society who of course had vested interests in the continuation of the Empire with its institutionalised racism, felt that Dyer was a hero, a military man who fully understood that the grumbling natives must be shown a lesson to spare 'everyone' from further bloodshed.

In the past, Dyer was often cast as a lone wolf, perhaps a tad trigger-happy when feeling outnumbered and presented with a situation beyond his control. Was he reckless perhaps? Lacking in self control, as often demonstrated throughout his life, a man who grew up without his parents' full love and attention, and one who became frustrated by his lack of active service and promotion in the military? It's certainly easier for us to believe that this act was one taken in isolation and then explained away or covered up (depending on your opinion) at a later date to protect 'one of our own'. After all, what could outsiders know of life in British India?

Unfortunately, Dyer did not act alone, or without several hours of consideration. He had a chain of command that, while not always communicating perfectly, gave at least a nod of approval to him to come down hard on the natives, and one that allowed similar behaviour to go unchecked in Amritsar for some months. What we would now recognise as racism was endemic in the British army in India, the Indian Civil Service and British Indian society as a whole at that time. Many of those expats who lived and worked in India truly believed that an Indian was not as 'civilised' or capable as a white man (or woman). Such opinions led the administration to arrange society in a way that only allowed the British the right to exert political influence and to prosper. And the sentiments were echoed back in Britain to some extent, where ruling the Empire was seen as the 'white man's burden', casting the imperialists in the role of caring benefactor. Of course, the 'Jewel in the Crown' offered far, far more to the British than just the opportunity to help out a lesser race. If we accept Dyer was officially sanctioned in his methods of dealing with those Indians calling for more political freedom, then we must accept that he acted on behalf of the British army, the Raj and effectively, although implicitly, the British government. And of course, if Britain had responded effectively at the time, we might not be here, one hundred years on, discussing the Amritsar massacre still.

To say that any official response was slow regarding the Jallianwala Bagh shooting is an understatement. Dyer himself dragged his heels waiting six hours before sending a short report back to his superiors, and those above him were less than responsive when he did. Details of the event were slow to emerge, and for a long time, casualties were thought to be far fewer, a particular embarrassment to Edwin Montagu,

Secretary of State for India back in England. It took concerted efforts by the native press, high profile Indians such as Rabindranath Tagore and later pressure from Montagu to elicit an official investigation from the Government of India. Dyer's first official report was submitted on 25 August, while the Hunter Committee only began in October. And both the Viceroy and Montagu used the Inquiry as a way to further delay their own responses, almost hoping any controversy would blow over. A more speedy reaction that showed the administration was concerned about the events may have gone some way to reassure the masses that the Raj did not accept this approach, and in turn respected the rights of the people within its territory.

Tardiness aside, another stumbling block on the road to repaired relationships was the final outcome of the Hunter Committee's work and how it was received. Despite an attempt at balance within the Committee members, a united decision was never forthcoming. This lack of consensus opened up further debate and the Viceroy's Legislative Council struggled to agree on how Dyer should now be dealt with. Legally, Dyer had never faced a trial, and yet he was to be punished by the loss of his job and future prospects within the army. The authorities had backed themselves into a corner, and this mishandling allowed Dyer and his supporters to mount an extended campaign to clear his name. It also brought dissention in the British parliament, with some appalled at Dyer's use of terror tactics (as was now his defence) and others unprepared to put native opinions above that of a British officer doing his duty, real or imagined. The Army Council also wanted to protect an officer, whatever the circumstance. Extended and emotional debates in response to Dyer's return to England, and the future he would face, effectively ended both Montagu's career and the tenure of the coalition government.

However, the focus remained fixed upon how fair it was to punish Dyer and the message that would send to British observers, rather than what the effect *of not* punishing those who took part in and sanctioned the shootings and events that followed, would have on India itself. This was an incredibly shortsighted approach and reinforces the belief that the British Raj simply did not care about its servants. Indians came, and always would come, a very poor second to Europeans. Another opportunity for contrition was missed.

But how could the Viceroy, the Government of India and the British government have responded better at the time to avoid the necessity to now revisit this chain of events over and over? Certainly, there should have been a speedier investigation – and determination of the major facts – such as how many casualties there were. There should also have been a clear investigation process laid out in advance, and one with evidence taken from both sides. This investigation should have been designed in such a way that a verdict was forthcoming at the end, so that there was a 'final' decision. The authority of the investigation to punish those it found lacking should also have been addressed at its formation. A formal admission that mistakes were made and apology from the authorities at the time could have prevented a deterioration of the relationship between the British and its subjects. It certainly would have maintained the working relationship between some nationalist leaders and the government. It might even have ensured a cleaner handover when the time came as the British Liberal government was committed to eventual Indian independence.

Some would argue however that the events at Amritsar pale into insignificance against other colonial crimes in India. In 1943, for example, up to four million Bengalis starved to death when Winston Churchill diverted food to British soldiers and countries such as Greece as a deadly famine swept through Bengal. There is also the retention of the Koh-I-Noor diamond, ceded to Queen Victoria when the East India Company took control of the Punjab. The governments of India, Pakistan, Iran, and Afghanistan have all claimed ownership since Indian independence. Consider, too, the Partition between India and the newly created state of Pakistan, which led to sectarian killings and an estimated death toll up to one million. It was allocated just six weeks of work, with some decisions rumoured to have been decided (or forced) over a single lunch. Sir Cyril Radcliffe was responsible for dividing the vast territories, which saw some fourteen million people — roughly seven million from each side — flee across the border when they discovered the new boundaries left them in the 'wrong' country. After seeing the bloody fallout, Radcliffe refused his salary of 40,000 rupees (then worth about £3,000). Christopher Beaumont was private secretary to Radcliffe, and in 2007 his personal papers came to light, in which he suggested Viceroy Mountbatten put pressure on Radcliffe to alter the boundary in India's favour, bent the rules and that the handover of power was carried out too quickly. Even now, Partition is blamed for poisoning relations between India and Pakistan, and interestingly, the first museum devoted to Partition opened in 2016 in Amritsar. This museum also currently houses an exhibition covering the Punjab's contribution to the struggle for freedom, which commemorates the Jallianwala Bagh massacre.

Considering these events, why is an apology for the Amritsar massacre such a sticking point? Perhaps it is because the shooting and more importantly its aftermath – and the British Indian response to both – showcases everything that was wrong with the Empire. So rather than being the very worst atrocity, it is one that stands for so much more. Indeed, some might argue that apologising for a single event is a mistake because contrition should be for the damage imperialism wrought as a whole. Many would also like to see a more accurate and thorough teaching of the Empire's history in UK's schools before an apology is offered so that the need to say sorry is actually understood by the populace now offering it on behalf of their predecessors.

So, should the British government formally apologise now because it failed to do so at the time? It certainly wouldn't be the only British apology covering its colonial past. In 1997, the Prime Minister Tony Blair expressed regret over British indifference to the plight of the Irish people during the potato famine of the 1840s. And in 2006, ahead of the 200th anniversary of the outlawing of the slave trade on British ships, Blair apologised and described the practice as 'profoundly shameful'. A few years later, in 2010, David Cameron apologised for the actions of British soldiers after the 'Bloody Sunday' Saville Inquiry found that fourteen civil rights demonstrators and bystanders were killed without justification.

Other nations and leaders too have apologized for their actions – and even their inactions – in the past. One of the most significant modern examples of a public apology was when, in 1970, the German Chancellor Willy Brandt fell to his knees in front of a Holocaust memorial in Warsaw. It was the first official German visit to Poland since the war, and through it Germany faced its past so that it could renew relationships with the country. In 1998, American President Bill Clinton apologised for the world's inaction during the genocide in Rwanda and F.W. de Klerk, who served as State President of South Africa from 1989 to 1994, apologised to the Truth and Reconciliation Commission for apartheid. In 1995, French President Jacques Chirac apologised for the help the Vichy government gave the Nazis in deporting French Jews to death camps and Boris Yeltsin apologised for the mistakes of the Bolshevik Revolution on its eightieth anniversary in 1997. In 1996, Japan's prime minister, Morihiro Hosokawa, described the Second World War as 'a mistake' and spoke of 'deep remorse and apologies for the fact that our country's past acts of aggression and colonial rule caused unbearable suffering and sorrow'. Pope John Paul II apologised for many things throughout the 1980s and 1990s on behalf of the Catholic Church, including the Crusades, the Inquisition, the oppression of women and the Holocaust. He believed that you can't 'heal the present, without making amends for the past'.

More recently, in 2016, Canadian Prime Minister Justin Trudeau apologised to the descendants of passengers of the Komagata Maru, a Japanese vessel that was carrying 376 Sikh, Muslim, and Hindu passengers that were denied entry into Canada in 1914 under immigration laws. This was the first in a series of formal apologies made by Trudeau's Liberal government to acknowledge historic injustices in the country's past. In 2008, Australia's Prime Minister Kevin Rudd apologized to the 'stolen generations', indigenous children who were forcibly removed from their families from the 1900s until as late as 1970.

But many of these apologies are harshly criticised. Broadcaster and journalist Jeremy Paxman was particularly disparaging about Blair's contrition, arguing that apologising for things that your forbearers did was 'a complete exercise in moral vacuousness'. This view would then hold that you could only apologise and have it mean something, if you carried out the act. Clearly that isn't possible with any historic acts, and perhaps it is a bit foolish (or headline grabbing?) to suggest it. Others are more cynical, believing these apologies only come when there is a political – or economic – reason that the leader of a nation may want to avoid more criticisms further down the line or patch up relations with an old foe or former friend. Never has that been more applicable than as Britain looks for favourable trade deals post-Brexit.

But should we look more sympathetically upon the modern move – some might even say the trend – to apologise? Can an apology be the best way to heal complex historical wounds by breaking the cycle of anger and revenge? Symbolically, saying sorry can be a powerful tool in redressing historical injustices and moving on from darker times. If the past leaves a legacy of distrust and conflict, a public apology can help prepare the path to reconciliation. Certainly there have been calls for both the queen and the British Government to apologise for atrocities from Britain's colonial past including the 1919 Amritsar massacre by controversial Indian MP and member of the All Indian Congress Party Shashi Tharoor. His best-selling book *Inglorious Empire: What the British did to India* grew from an Oxford Union debate in 2015 that argued that Britain should pay India symbolic reparations because of the damage inflicted by the British. He cites famines, the policy of 'divide and conquer' and protectionist trade regulations that built England's commerce at the expense of India's. He notes that after two centuries of British Rule, India's share of the world economy had decreased six-fold. Each Imperial 'gift', he believes, came with a hefty price tag that the natives paid.

Mayor of London Sadiq Khan supports the call for the British government to make a formal apology for the Jallianwala Bagh massacre. He raised the issue on a 2017 visit to Amritsar's Golden Temple, calling the event one of the most horrific events in Indian history. Khan believes an apology – particularly as the centenary nears – would acknowledge what happened and give the people of Amritsar and India the closure they need. And in 2018, close to the ninety-ninth anniversary of the massacre, MP for Ealing Southall, Virendra Sharma, called for a permanent memorial in London and for the massacre and all aspects of colonialism to be taught as part of the national curriculum. Sharma has previously submitted an Early Day Motion, calling upon Theresa May to apologise for the atrocities in Amritsar.

In 1997, Queen Elizabeth visited the Jallianwala Bagh during a state visit, and took the time to lay a wreath at the memorial. But while she described the event as a 'distressing example' of a difficult episode from our past, she did not apologise formally. Similarly, David Cameron visited as Prime Minister in 2013, also placing a wreath at the memorial. He signed the visitor's book, calling the shooting 'a deeply shameful event' and referencing Winston Churchill's use of the term 'monstrous', but again stopped short of anything more, stating that he did not think it was the right thing 'to reach back into history and to seek out things you can apologise for'. This caused the Indian journalist Sankarshan Thakur to write wryly in the *Daily Telegraph* 'Over nearly a century now British protagonists have approached the 1919 massacre ground of Jallianwala Bagh thumbing the thesaurus for an appropriate word to pick. "Sorry" has not been among them'. In 2016, Prince William and the Duchess of Cambridge sidestepped the issue when they left the site out of their itinerary as they toured the country.

And what of the argument that Britain also gave India as much as it took; a free press, democracy, the rule of law, an effective railway system and the 'international' language of English? Again, many would argue that these were by-products of the exploitative relationship India endured with the Raj, rather than carefully considered endowments. When Gandhi turned his back on the British way of life that had been imposed upon his country it was because he felt India had its own traditions, stretching back to ancient civilisations, and he believed the future of his country lay in reviving this way of life, rather than adopting the values of another nation. It's also worth noting that, on a practical level alone, India paid for the civil service, the army, infrastructure and the many other 'gifts' it hadn't asked for in heavy taxes, while most of the wealth from salaries went back to England with those that had worked a stint in the colony.

Since 2013 however, politics in the UK has changed dramatically. Originally David Cameron came to power in 2010 in the first coalition government in the UK since Churchill's Conservative-led coalition that lasted for most of the Second World War. The Conservative party was voted in again in 2015 but this time with a majority. The following year, the UK voted on a referendum on EU membership, and the leave party gained a narrow win with 51.9 per cent of the votes. Having campaigned to remain in the EU, Cameron immediately resigned, perhaps all too aware that this was the first time a national referendum result had gone against the preferred option of the UK government. Home Secretary Theresa May took over as leader of the Conservative party and Prime Minister, and a further general election was called in 2017, with Theresa May staying in her new role to run a minority Conservative government. It's fair to say it has been a tumultuous time and many aspects of the Brexit deal still remain unclear at the time of writing. And while we negotiate trade deals with our former EU colleagues, we also need to look further afield to our relationships beyond Europe.

Would it be wrong to apologise as we enter this new era of international relations? Perhaps yes, if our doing so stems entirely from the desire to put in place profitable deals across the globe. But what if the period we are now entering is also an opportunity to put our collective ignorance and amnesia about the truth of colonialism (good and bad) into context and move towards a more modern moral respectability within global interactions? Post-Brexit, we may well find we are redefining our understanding of what 'being British' means. In the past, any inhabitant of the Empire – whether white or non-white, from Britain or not – could at one point have been considered 'British'. Those in the Commonwealth may also have had an identity based on their 'Britishness'. But what are the qualities that bind our countrymen to us in the twenty-first century, and are there any? Do we consider ourselves British, European or global citizens? Is it important to our national identity now that we can acknowledge mistakes of the past, and show compassion for them, even if that's an uncomfortable experience?

During the Raj, British identity was caught up with a sense of military honour, fair play through an organised justice system and the emotional detachment of retaining the 'stiff upper lip'. The British upper class, with their ethno-centric sense of superiority ruled the Raj, bringing with them ethics drawn from their hereditary privilege and upbringing, and the lower social classes that moved to India for work and advancement accepted and aspired to their way of life. But back in England the middle classes – who had earned their wealth through hard work and business acumen – were beginning to change society. The early twentieth century had brought Liberal welfare reforms and compulsory state-run education, and increasingly social mobility was becoming possible. In British India, those who had gained their elevated status simply by birth wanted to retain the traditions that had placed them at the top of the heap, not change society for the betterment of all. This why the aristocracy the Raj favoured, fought long and hard to retain the Empire, because they also wanted to retain their superior status within it.

At the end of the day, perhaps we should balance what would happen if Britain apologised for the Jallianwala Bagh shooting as the 100th anniversary approaches, versus what would happen if it chose not to. If Britain allows the centenary to pass by unacknowledged, it risks being viewed as defensive and arrogant – perhaps with a fragile sense of self – and unwilling even to listen to some of its own citizens. Agreed, some might argue that an apology could open the door to calls for further contrition concerning other events – or even financial claims – although the latter is unlikely (more likely any cost in this instance would be covered by taking responsibility for a suitable memorial). But ultimately is it more damaging to be seen as a nation that refuses to face its past mistakes?

An apology, however, could bring healing to the descendants (including citizens of the UK, India and Pakistan) of those that suffered in the Punjab and it could open the path to cultural and economic relations with India, other former colonies, the Commonwealth and beyond. It would also give a clear signal that the Britain of the twenty-first century is an open and sympathetic nation, with its eyes on the future and not the past. And going forward, surely that is how Britain wants to be perceived?

Conclusion

When I first learnt about the Amritsar Massacre of 1919 I thought it an indefensible act carried out, I assumed, by a battle-weary white man with a superiority complex and a sense of entitlement I could little understand. However, while the Jallianwala Bagh shooting remains indefensible, I've come to realise that Reginald Dyer and his actions on 13 April represent so much more than an isolated incident of inhumanity at the hands of a British army officer. And perhaps far more important than Dyer's motivation for the killings was the response to them – and the lack thereof – which far many more people are guilty of. The fact that he and those others who could also be held to account for the incident were never punished is why this atrocity remains an open wound, and why it is so significant in any understanding of the history of the British Raj.

Reginald Dyer was typical of his day and of his class. A British boy born to well-off, if not well-to-do, parents in India, that grew up enjoying all it had to offer. Before he became a man however, he was sent away from his *ayah* and Hindustani servants to a boarding school in Ireland during a period of local political upheaval, immediately becoming a fish out of water. His desire it seems was always to return to India and join the army there, which he worked hard to fulfill. Dyer managed to rise in the ranks of the Indian Army – sometimes cutting corners to do so – and he was popular with the troops he commanded, including native soldiers. His career was mixed and although he didn't always follow orders he was still a decorated and experienced officer by the time he was left in charge of the city of Amritsar. Because of this is it unrealistic to suggest that his actions on the 13th were based on fear. In fact he was well-versed in military strategy and had plenty of time to plan and prepare for the crowds he knew had assembled in Jallianwala Bagh.

Despite his obvious love for India, or rather the India he believed existed, Dyer held certain opinions common at that time. The first was that the British had every right to be in charge of India and Indians and that it was best for the natives that the British were there to protect and guide them. It was not unusual for the British living in India and those back at home to believe that non-whites were uncivilised people, unable to organise and maintain a functioning society. The British brought to the colonies law and order, education and sanitation and commerce. In reality of course, India, like many other imperial lands, actually afforded its invaders rich pickings and as time progressed an import/export business that lined the pockets of all those involved (except the natives) and a vast nation of people to put to work and war.

Accordingly, Dyer, and those of his ilk, regarded Indians as inferior and expected them to respect the supposed superiority of the British military. Part of the story at Amritsar was that across the Punjab, nationalists and others were beginning to question the autocratic rule of Britain and they showed this growing awareness by refusing to do as they were told. The India Dyer and his compatriots knew was changing, even Liberal politicians back in England were talking of reform and self-rule. When Dyer arrived in Amritsar on 11 April, he had been told of the riots and violence that had occurred and was keen to put the rebels in their place. He was no doubt irked by the lack of respect he personally received as he paraded his men through the city streets to read his proclamation. When he learned that many planned to disobey his orders against mass gatherings, he was clearly determined to come down hard on the agitators. And he did.

But Dyer was not unsupported in the devastation he caused. His superior officers – and in particular Michael O'Dwyer – also subscribed to the view that the natives must be taught a lesson. Some might argue that the massacre at Amritsar, which was preceded by several days of peace was less of a reaction to an unauthorised meeting and more of a revenge attack for the crimes committed after the deportation of Kitchlew and Satya Pal, which included the murder and physical assault of British men and women, and the arson, looting and vandalism of the buildings and property that symbolised the British Raj. Men such as Dyer and O'Dwyer thought they were fighting a war, and losing sight of the fact that those gathered in the Jallianwala Bagh were unarmed civilians, many unconnected in to the previous violence the city had experienced, Amritsar was their battlefield.

More damaging than the event itself however, was the way in which it was dealt with, both immediately and in the longer term. To begin with there were only conservative estimates of casualties – and short reports. The British army and the Indian Government stood side by side as they downplayed events. Their message was clear – those in authority in British India did not have to explain themselves and their actions – and particularly not if the natives were demanding that explanation. Those of a Liberal persuasion back in England didn't understand the colonial lifestyle – or the native and his need to be firmly put down. Of course, the value system of the Raj was flawed. Only in British India could a far lower price (500 rupees) be put on the head of an Indian killed at the Jallianwala Bagh than that of a European murdered in the violence on the 10th (the widow of Mr Stewart the murdered bank manager was awarded 20,000 rupees).

While an official investigation of the events in the Punjab and at Jallianwala Bagh could have begun the healing process, the Hunter Committee and its official report proved to be exactly the opposite. Here, Dyer was able to change his story, pass off the idea of making an example of the crowds in Amritsar in order that other rebels might be deterred without criticism and suggest his actions actually spared bloodshed. Evidence was taken only from the government of India and the likely underreported figure of 379 dead was accepted despite the crowd in the enclosed park being as many as twenty thousand strong. O'Dwyer even had the cheek to complain about how Indian committee members were allowed to question him.

The lack of consensus achieved by the Committee, and the obvious racial bias of members coupled with no practical punishments for those censured made a mockery of the process. When the Report reached the British Government, it too failed to act definitively, and India was shocked to see so many supporters for the establishment. Justice – that value the colonialists claimed to adhere to so very much – was far from served. And while Dyer didn't get off without the loss of his job, neither was he formally disciplined either by the Army or the courts. Criticised and with a reduced income yes, but still able to revel in his role as 'the saviour of the Punjab'. And when he died, Dyer was treated like a hero.

The real significance of Amritsar however became the ultimate punishment for the British Raj. After the shooting – and following the lack of reparations – the fragile relationship between the Indian Government and those she governed was broken beyond repair. For many it proved beyond doubt that the British did not care for their Indian subjects and that their sense of fair play was just an illusion. Congress President Pandit Motilal Nehru, father of Jawaharlal Nehru, the first Prime Minister of India, called the massacre the 'saddest and most revealing of all'. Widespread support grew for nationalism and its leaders no longer accepted a gradual move to increased involvement in the administration, instead demanding freedom for the people of India. While it would take twenty-eight years before independence came, the Jallianwala massacre made it inevitable.

In the 100 years since the shooting, Britain has missed many opportunities to apologise for its actions that day and the period of punitive martial law imposed directly after. Both the queen and Prime Minister David Cameron visited the area in 1997 and 2013 respectively and sidestepped the issue. Of course, an apology could be conceived as complex – the events in Amritsar are not the only atrocity Britain could be held to account for. An apology by today's heads of state and government representatives could also be considered meaningless as they are not directly responsible for the action taken in 1919. Indeed, when the Queen was criticised for not offering an apology, the then Prime Minister of India Inder Kumar Gujral defended her, saying that since she had not even been born at the time of the events, she should not be required to say sorry.

The Amritsar Massacre was a pivotal point in Indian history, bringing in a new era that would result in national independence and the creation of Pakistan. While the shooting was a monstrous act in itself, the real atrocity was the continued subjection of a country demanding political change and the trivialising of the methods used to put down the people of India. There were many ways for the British to demonstrate it would make good on the Liberal government's promise to hand power back to India, the way agitation in Amritsar was dealt with in 1919 was not one of them.

Is an apology offered today meaningless? Perhaps yes, if it is done so without a full understanding of what is represents, as such an apology would be an empty gesture if offered simply to placate critics. This is why UK politicians such as the MP for Ealing Southall Virendra Sharma and London Mayor Sadiq Khan don't only seek an apology but rather want the history of the Empire taught in British schools as part of the national curriculum. In this way, future generations can shake off the romantic and vague idea of what the British Raj was like – and understand fully the implications of an imperialist past. Only then can society look forward to improved international relations.

Bibliography

CHADHA, Yogesh, *Rediscovering Gandhi* Arrow Books, London, 1998

COATES, Tim (Series Editor), *Uncovered editions: The Amritsar Massacre, 1919. General Dyer in the Punjab* The Stationery Office, London, 2000

COLLETT, Nigel, *The Butcher of Amritsar: General Reginald Dyer* Hambledon and London, London, 2005

DRAPER, Alfred, *Echoes of War: The Amritsar Massacre, Twilight of the Raj* Buchan & Enright Publishers, London, 1985

FURNEAUX, Rupert, *Massacre at Amritsar* George Allen & Unwin Ltd, London, 1963

GUHA, Ramachandra, *Gandhi before India* Penguin Books, London, 2014

HABIB, S. Irfan (Editor), *Indian Nationalism: The Essential Writings* Aleph Book Company, New Delhi, 2017

HERMAN, Arthur, *Gandhi & Churchill: the epic rivalry that destroyed an empire and forged our age* Hutchinson, London, 2008

JUDD, Denis, *The Lion and the Tiger: The rise and fall of the British Raj* Oxford University Press, Oxford, 2004

KHAN, Yasmin, *The Great Partition: The Making of India and Pakistan* Yale University Press, New Haven and London, 2007

MASSELOS, Jim, *Indian Nationalism: An History* Oriental University Press, London, 1986

NANDA, B.R. *Gokhale, Gandhi and the Nehrus: Studies in Indian Nationalism* George Allen & Unwin Ltd, London, 1974

THAROOR, Shashi, *Inglorious Empire: What the British did to India* Hurst & Company, London, 2017

Index